"One of the best ways we can tack[...] at a time, empowering women with acce[...] he economic opportunity they need and deserve. This compelling and wise collection of essays tells you how to join the fight."

— **President William J. Clinton**

"I began to cry after about five minutes of reading, and didn't stop till I put the book down, equal parts heartbreak and gratitude—heartbreak because I'm a mom, and the realities that mothers and children experience globally are unspeakable, and gratitude for the brave and intelligent people that God is using right these wrongs. A hopeful, important, inspiring book."

— **Shauna Niequist,** Author of *Bread & Wine*

"If you want to improve the welfare of a country, you must uplift the caliber and character of the healthcare available to mothers and children, the very life force of a nation and key to its longevity. *The Mother & Child Project* uniquely explains how each of us can participate in changing the access to healthcare for women and children around the world."

— **Bishop T.D. Jakes,** The Potter's House

"Every child deserves a healthy mother. And every mother deserves a healthy child. If only the world were that simple. The stories in the *The Mother & Child Project* offer a window into the struggles of families worldwide when people lack access to health care, nutrition, and education. The good news is that we can do something; we can help change lives. Be inspired to get involved as you read the powerful words in this book."

— **Sheryl Crow,** Grammy-Award Winning
Singer and Songwriter

"The progress the world has seen against poverty, preventable child deaths, mothers dying in childbirth is nothing short of miraculous. But progress' evil twin is complacency, a tired sense all will be well. The Mother and Child Project is the clarion call to ensure we finish the job, until mothers have what they need to raise healthy families and no child dies for lack of vaccines and medicines we can get at any pharmacy."

— **Michael Elliott,** President and CEO, ONE

"Few things in life are as important as a healthy family, and around the world today that often starts with the flourishing lives of women and children. This must-read book illustrates why maternal and child health are of such crucial importance for this—and future—generations. It could be your first step to offering hope for millions."

—**Richard Stearns,** President of World Vision US and
author of *The Hole in Our Gospel* and *Unfinished*

"From introductions by Kay Warren and Melinda Gates ... to stellar chapters from a who's-who in Christian thought and leadership ... to helpful how-to appendices at the end, this book will help you understand why helping mothers and children is key to making the world a better place. And more: you'll learn how you can get involved, right where you are, to make people's lives better everywhere.

—**Brian D. McLaren,** Author and Speaker

"God calls us all to serve as advocates for the poor, the marginalized, and the disenfranchised, at home and around the world. *The Mother & Child Project* calls us not just to speak up, but to take action on behalf of millions of young women and children in developing nations. In the health of these women and children rests the promise of a better future for everyone."

—**Lynne Hybels,** Advocate for Global Engagement
Willow Creek Community Church

"Mothers and children are at the heart of vulnerability of extreme poverty and diseases, like HIV/AIDS, tuberculosis, and malaria. *The Mother & Child Project* describes ways in which you can get involved to help moms around the world have a better chance at surviving pregnancy and childbirth and help kids thrive in their early years. This strong start can provide a solid foundation for families to have happier, healthier lives.

—**Dr. Mark Dybul,** Executive Director of the Global Fund

The
Mother
&Child
Project

Also Read

The aWAKE Project:
Uniting Against the African AIDS Crisis

The Mother &Child Project

RAISING OUR VOICES *for* HEALTH AND HOPE

Compiled by
Hope Through Healing Hands

ZONDERVAN

The Mother and Child Project
Copyright © 2015 by Zondervan

This title is also available as a Zondervan ebook. Visit www.zondervan.com/ebooks.

Requests for information should be addressed to:
Zondervan, 3900 *Sparks Drive SE, Grand Rapids, Michigan 49546*

ISBN 978-0-310-34161-1

All Scripture quotations, unless otherwise indicated, are taken from The Holy Bible, *New International Version®, NIV®.* Copyright © 1973, 1978, 1984, 2011 by Biblica, Inc.® Used by permission. All rights reserved worldwide.

Scripture quotations marked MSG are taken from *THE MESSAGE.* Copyright © by Eugene Peterson 1993, 1994, 1995, 1996, 2000, 2001, 2002. Used by permission of NavPress Publishing Group.

Scripture quotations marked NLT are taken from the *Holy Bible, New Living Translation,* copyright © 1996, 2004, 2007 by Tyndale House Foundation. Used by permission of Tyndale House Publishers, Inc., Carol Stream, Illinois 60188. All rights reserved.

The views expressed in the essays in this book are those of the essays' individual authors and do not reflect the views of the editors, the publisher, or the other essayists. The editors have listed organizations in the Resources section that they think are useful, but these listings should not be construed as an endorsement of the organizations. The editors and publisher have no connection with these organizations and accept no liability for the advice, acts, or omissions of these organizations.

Any Internet addresses (websites, blogs, etc.) and telephone numbers in this book are offered as a resource. They are not intended in any way to be or imply an endorsement by Zondervan, nor does Zondervan vouch for the content of these sites and numbers for the life of this book.

All rights reserved. No part of this publication may be reproduced, stored in a retrieval system, or transmitted in any form or by any means — electronic, mechanical, photocopy, recording, or any other — except for brief quotations in printed reviews, without the prior permission of the publisher.

Compiled by Jenny Eaton Dyer, PhD, Kate Etue, and Hope Through Healing Hands

Cover design: Dual Identity
Cover photography: Esther Havens
Interior photography: Unless noted below, © World Vision, Inc. 2014. *All Rights Reserved.*
    Stephanie May Wilson, pages 16, 129, 140, 151, 158, 164, 208
    Brianna L. Danese, pages 128, 172, 179, 202
Interior design: Kait Lamphere

First Printing February 2015 / Printed in the United States of America

For the 287,000 women who lost their lives last year due to complications in pregnancy or childbirth.

And for the 220 million women around the world awaiting the education and services to time and space their next pregnancy in a healthy way.

We lift up your voices.
Because no mother should fear the birth of her child.

Contents

Part 4:
Why Maternal Health Matters to People of Faith

Foreword

Choosing Joy for Mothers and Children

Kay Warren

◄❍►

For more than a decade, God has taken me on a journey. A journey in which I had to walk by faith, not by sight. I didn't know where God was leading me, and I wasn't sure I was ready to follow. But I did. I followed God to corners of the world I never imagined I would ever visit: places like Cambodia, Mozambique, and Rwanda. God called me out of my insulated suburban life in Southern California, opening my eyes to the painful reality of those in the most dire of circumstances — orphans, those living with HIV and AIDS, and those in extreme poverty.

Upon this journey I have come to know the suffering of mothers and children with many faces and many names. I have listened with a broken heart to stories of violence against women and children and stories of mothers dying in childbirth. I have met orphaned children caring for their orphaned siblings and have met children in the care of their grandmothers because their parents had died of HIV and AIDS.

These people and these stories matter.

Today I write for *The Mother and Child Project* because God calls us to "speak up for those who cannot speak for themselves" (Proverbs 31:8). Last year, more than 6.6 million children under the age of five died from preventable, treatable causes. Many of these children died in the arms of loving parents who simply didn't have access to basic newborn care, simple antibiotics, vaccines, or oral rehydration therapies. For pennies to the dollar, these children's lives could have been saved. In addition, more than 287,000 women died last year in childbirth. They died because they lacked a skilled attendant during birth and had complications during pregnancy or delivery.

The good news is that we know how to prevent these needless tragic deaths. The challenge is to choose to do so.

The nexus of global health issues revolves around the stability of the family, especially the mother and child. If the mother can remain healthy and happy and stable, the family can flourish physically, socially, economically, and spiritually. When families gain the skills to plan the timing and spacing of their children, and when mothers have access to prenatal care, lives will be saved. Then other global health issues can be tackled. We can begin to combat extreme poverty, keep young girls and children in school, promote gender equality, improve maternal and child health, and fight infectious diseases like HIV and AIDS.

In the developing world, too many mothers are losing their children to preventable, treatable causes. Likewise, too many children are losing their mothers due to complications in pregnancy and birth that could easily be avoided.

In 2013, I, too, became a mother who lost her child.

I empathize and resonate with the intense grief of such a precious, tragic loss.

I stand by these millions of women and children in their loss around the world to say that in the midst of mourning, we can choose to do something. We, as Americans, can choose to prevent these deaths with our personal and governmental support for maternal, newborn, and child health and healthy timing and spacing of pregnancies in ways that honor God. Our voices can and will make a difference.

And, in doing so, we choose joy.

Kay Warren is the co-founder of Saddleback Church, wife of pastor Rick Warren, an author and Christian communicator, and an advocate for people struggling with mental illness. She and her husband live in Lake Forest, California.

Preface

All Lives Have Equal Value

Melinda Gates

◄O►

I grew up in a Catholic family. One of the earliest lessons instilled by my teachers at Ursuline Academy was that all people have boundless dignity. That lesson stuck; today it's the source of the Gates Foundation's guiding principle: "All lives have equal value."

These days, as a co-chair of the foundation, my teachers are the women—mothers and wives, daughters and sisters—I meet when I travel to developing countries. The lessons they teach are about what connects all people—that we all want to provide for our families and give our children a better future.

My favorite part of my job is talking to these women about what they need to create that better future. One topic they talk about all the time is high-quality health care.

To help women and children fulfill their potential, we need to make sure they can receive the right kind of health care at every phase of their lives. Each aspect of reproductive, maternal, newborn, and child health connects to the next. To take one example, when women plan for healthy timing and spacing of pregnancies, they are more likely to be healthy, and they are more likely to have healthier babies. Healthy babies are more likely to grow up strong and become productive adults. It's a virtuous cycle.

In short, the challenge for us is to strengthen all of the links on the chain that leads to a thriving future. And when we empower women to get great care along this continuum, they in turn compound those investments by reinvesting in those around them.

Time and time again, I have listened to women explain what they need to help their children flourish, including timing and spacing their pregnancies in healthy ways. That's why I decided to publicly champion access to family planning, including contraceptives. I've also focused on improving the other parts of the continuum so that every link in that chain is as strong as the next.

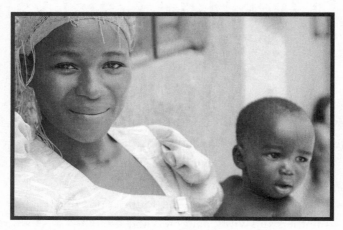

In doing this work, I've met so many inspiring colleagues. I've found that many global health professionals are driven by the same values that have guided me since Catholic school. And I've seen that people of faith and faith-based organizations, with their strong commitment to helping their neighbors, are an essential part of the development community. In fact, I've been working for years with faith-based organizations to promote health and prosperity for women and children. We are all natural allies based on our shared belief in the value of every human being.

I am honored to share common ground with the essayists in *The Mother and Child Project*. The journeys that have led each of them to lend their voice on behalf of mothers and their children are yet another source for my own inspiration—as I hope they are for you.

Melinda Gates is co-chair of the Bill & Melinda Gates Foundation.

Introduction

When the conversation about HIV/AIDS relief began at the turn of the millennium, the dialogue was complicated, particularly among people of faith. AIDS had been a key issue in the culture wars. As the then-surgeon general Dr. C. Everett Koop said, "AIDS pitted the politics of the gay revolution of the seventies against the politics of the Reagan revolution of the eighties." When the Barna Group polled evangelicals in 2001 to ask whether they would be willing to donate money to help children orphaned by AIDS, only 3 percent answered that they definitely would.

But times have changed. Thanks to heroic leadership in the faith community from Rick and Kay Warren, Bill and Lynne Hybels, Franklin Graham, Bishop T. D. Jakes, Bishop Charles E. Blake, Tony Campolo, Rich Stearns, Jim Wallis, Brian McLaren, Max Lucado, Michael W. Smith, Jars of Clay, and many, many other leading influencers, the language began to change. Hearts began to change. And the church began to rethink its position on HIV/AIDS, at home and around the world.

Fifteen years later, we celebrate the turning of the tide against AIDS. The past decade showcased a historic initiative to fight a single virus: HIV/AIDS, a disease that has hollowed out societies in Africa. In 2002, fewer than 50,000 people in Africa had access to antiretroviral medication (ARVs), but today more than 12.9 million people have access to lifesaving ARVs in developing nations. This is a cause for celebration. With the collaboration of voices of citizens and activists across the United States, presidential leadership, congressional bipartisanship, celebrity advocacy, and nonprofit coalitions, the United States, through the President's Emergency Plan For AIDS Relief (PEPFAR) and the Global Fund to Fight AIDS, Tuberculosis and Malaria, has and is saving the lives of millions. But we are rethinking our focus in global health. There are other millennium development goals to achieve and millions of lives that could be saved with simple interventions.

Another historic initiative is taking place today, in the fight to save the lives of mothers and children. *The Mother and Child Project: Raising Our Voices for Health and Hope* is a collection of essays written by artists and actors, nurses and doctors, policymakers and pastors highlighting the spectrum of concerns for mothers and children around the world. We want to educate the reader on the critical importance that healthy timing and spacing of pregnancies (HTSP) plays to combat extreme poverty, keep girls and children in school, promote gender equality, improve maternal and child health, and prevent mother-to-child transmission of HIV/AIDS. We believe that HTSP, or family planning, is at the nexus of global health issues.

Each section of this book opens with the personal story of a woman living in a developing nation in Africa or Asia, and each shares her experience of marriage and children and daily life. These stories are based on the original writing or interviews of these women, who are eager to share their experiences and the importance of HTSP for their lives and the lives of their families.

Our hope is that the essays inspire the reader to action. Hope Through Healing Hands, as the compiler, offers an array of options for what you can do next. We welcome you to research these options for advocacy and involvement so that you can take part in saving the lives of millions of mothers and children around the world.

Third World Woman

Amy Grant

◄O►

What if I were that mother staring from my TV?
What if that were my brown-eyed baby
Hungry as she could be?
What if that were my family?
What if that was my world?
Waiting on water, waiting on a vaccine,
Waiting on someone to bring me a bag of beans.

Lord, have mercy on me,
Have mercy on me.

What if I was that mother and I was waiting on me,
The big success, so well-dressed,
On the other side of the sea,
Living with my distractions.
Life's been good to me.
Maybe she's praying,
Praying for a miracle.
Maybe the answer is me.

Lord, have mercy on me,
Have mercy on me.

I was born in Georgia, where I could do as I please,
And I can get my hands on just about
Anything I might need.
Who is that third world woman?
Who is she to me?
Could be mother, could be daughter, could be sister to me.

Lord, have mercy on me,
Have mercy on me.

Amy Grant is a Grammy Award–winning singer and songwriter. She lives in Nashville, Tennessee, with her husband, Vince Gill, and their children.

Part 1

Maternal and Child Health

How Healthy Timing and Spacing of Pregnancy Saves Lives

Mihret Gebrehiwot's Story
Ethiopia

I am Mihret Gebrehiwot, a health extension worker working at Gemad health post in the Tigray region of Ethiopia.

I am the first child in my family. I was born and grew up in a small village called Genfel, located near Wukro town. I spent most of my childhood playing games, singing, and dancing, until I got married. As the first child in the family, I was given much care. I was not given much work beyond my capacity—unlike others in rural villages. My family's living standard was relatively better than others as my father had an additional source of income besides agriculture. My parents were loving to each other, which was a lesson for me.

When I reached school age, I went to school in the same village until the sixth grade. In the elementary school, most of the time I achieved high grades and stood in the first three ranks in class. When I was a student, I was interested in science and dreamed of being a doctor. During group work, I preferred to play the role of a doctor.

When I was in grade three, I married at the age of twelve. Both of our families arranged the marriage, and the ceremony took place in church. My husband was a deacon (who studied church education). Frankly, neither of us was interested in marriage. We were young and still students, but we had no other option. From seventh to tenth grade, I had to travel to Wukro every day for school.

When I was sixteen, my menstruation did not return, and I learned that I was pregnant. I was too young, so I was praying to be safe until I delivered. I was also worried that my expected delivery coincided with the examination dates of the eighth grade national examination. My father was also worried and contacted the school director. The school director was positive and made arrangements for if my delivery actually happened at the same time. Fortunately, I delivered two days after the examination.

I now have two children, and I plan to have one more. Because I had reasonable spacing between the two deliveries, I was able to complete my schooling and secure a job. Had it not been so, I would have discontinued my education at grade eight and faced the problems that many uneducated women are facing.

Family planning gives the opportunity for a woman to achieve her plan in every aspect of life as she will get adequate time. Child spacing is very important. Currently, there is access to family planning information and services in Ethiopia through the health posts, like the one I work in.

Despite the problems in Ethiopia, we are working hard to change them, and we are appreciating the changes that are coming. I tell people from the United States that there is much improvement in Ethiopia in terms of women empowerment, and many lessons can be shared with the rest of the world about women actively participating in changing their lives.

I hope to do this with my first child. She is a girl. I always encourage her to be strong. I hope she will have a better future and serve her community.

Chapter 1

A Mama Knows

◄o► *Rachel Held Evans*

A mama knows . . .

A mama knows the difference between a playful coo and a hungry whimper, a real fever and a valiant attempt to get out of school. She can spot a secret in the curl of a smile, a lie in the shift of the eyes, an impending illness in the subtle tilt of a head. She knows the rhythms of the household — the patter of toddler feet on the floor, the hurried scratches of forks against empty plates, the sweet and steady sucking of a baby at the breast. And she knows the rhythms of her own body, when it is heavy with milk, sore from cramps, exhausted from labor, in need of rest. A mama knows when something isn't right.

A mama keeps a mental inventory of the resources, turning the numbers over in her mind at night, willing there to be enough food for each belly, enough money for the girls to go to school, enough medicine at the clinic, enough energy to get through the next day. She knows the weight of a baby in her womb and a toddler on her back and how it affects her ability to work in the fields, to walk miles to fetch clean water, to care for the others. A mama knows what is best for her family, and so a mama is strongest when she is empowered to make good decisions for them.

But not every woman gets to choose. Not every mama gets the chance to do what she knows is best for herself and her family. There are more than 220 million women in developing countries who don't want to get pregnant, but who lack access to the family planning information and contraceptives many of us take for granted. Every year, nearly 300,000 of them will die during pregnancy or from complications giving birth, and many more will be permanently disabled. Far too many mothers will bury their babies before they even get to know the sound of their laughter or the tenor of their cries. More than 2.6 million babies will be stillborn, and another 2.9 million will die before they are a month old.

Giving women the opportunity to time their pregnancies and space out their children through effective, low-cost contraception is key to turning these heartbreaking numbers around. In fact, some believe it could save as many as 2 million children every year. Not only does access to family planning information and contraception improve the health of mothers and children, but it also improves the economies of their households. When a woman has fewer children and more time to work harvesting crops or growing her fledgling business, she brings more resources into the home so her children can be fed and go to school. If a poor family must weather a drought or famine, they are more likely to survive with a smaller household and fewer mouths to feed.

These are things that every mother knows instinctively, and yet ensuring that every woman has access to the contraception options she wants is not always a top priority on the global health agenda.

That's because conversations about contraception, particularly here in the United States, tend to be religiously and politically charged. Some people seem to think that family planning is just code for abortion, when it's not. Others presume that giving women access to contraception is encouraging them to behave promiscuously, even though most of the women who use oral contraceptives are married. Still others get caught up in domestic debates over insurance coverage and religious freedom and who should pay for what. Words like *entitled, selfish,* and even *slut* get thrown around, our perspectives tragically skewed by our own luxury of choice.

But a woman who wants to live long enough to see her children grow up isn't being selfish. A woman who wants to provide an education for her girls as well as her boys isn't acting entitled. A woman who wants to space out her pregnancies so her newborns have a better shot at life isn't a slut. And we cannot allow simplistic, self-focused narratives about contraception and family planning to keep us from helping these women, from ensuring they have the opportunity to choose.

For those of us who identify as pro-life, it's not enough simply to oppose abortion. We must also actively advocate for and invest in those specific actions that not only curb the abortion rate but also save the lives of women and children worldwide. Increasing access to family planning information and contraceptives will result in fewer women and girls dying in pregnancy and childbirth, fewer unintended pregnancies, fewer abortions, and fewer infant deaths. This is why I am convinced that a consistent pro-life ethic must include promoting access to effective and affordable contraception. Millions of lives, of both the born and the unborn, are at stake.

> **For those of us who identify as pro-life, it's not enough simply to oppose abortion. We must also actively advocate for and invest in actions that save the lives of women and children worldwide.**

As Christians, we are called to reorient our perspective around the needs of the most vulnerable, those whom Jesus called "the least of these." But the truth is, when we lean in close, we learn that "the least of these" aren't all that different from ourselves. The mothers of sub-Saharan Africa chuckle the same way over the antics of their mischievous children as do mothers here in the United States. The women of Southeast Asia share the same instincts and intuition as women in Europe, women in South America, women from centuries past, and women from centuries to come.

A baby's death is no less tragic when it happens quietly on a dirt floor than when it happens in a high-tech hospital amid a web of ventilators and tubes. We may have dissimilar circumstances, but we share a common humanity, a shared dream of raising healthy and happy families.

Melinda Gates often tells the story of a Kenyan mother named Maryanne who spoke with Gates about her community's struggle to get access to contraception. "I want to bring every good thing to this child," Maryanne told her, "before I have another."

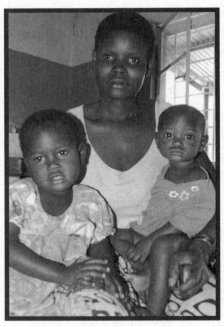

A mama knows.

A mama knows when it is time to grow a family and when it is time to wait. A mama knows how far the rations will stretch, how much school uniforms cost, how long she ought to nurse her baby. A mama knows when her body needs a rest. And a mama knows how to bring every good thing to that little boy whose head nestles into her soft, waiting shoulder.

Let's give her the chance to do it.

Rachel Held Evans is the author of Evolving in Monkey Town *and* A Year of Biblical Womanhood. *She lives in Dayton, Tennessee, with her husband, Dan.*

Chapter 2

Contraception Is a Pro-Life Cause in Developing World

◄○► *Bill Frist and Jenny Eaton Dyer*

When it comes to the health of children and mothers worldwide, there are immense challenges, yet many signs of hope.

Over 6.9 million children die every year in the developing world from preventable, treatable causes. While the loss of these children is a tragedy of epic proportions, the good news is that over the last six years, this number has been lowered by 35 percent. We know we *can* combat newborn mortality and enhance child survival. Simple, low-cost measures are being taken to ensure better health for these children around the world. Measures like oral rehydration therapy, bed nets to prevent malaria, and access to immunizations have accelerated the rate of reducing child mortality in developing nations.

With an increased focus on maternal, newborn, and child health over the past few years, the global community has seen real progress against daunting challenges. An underappreciated part of that story is healthy birth spacing and timing, or family planning, which has a profound effect on the survival and quality of life of both mothers and children. As Michael Gerson, former speechwriter for President George W. Bush and *Washington Post* columnist, puts it, "family planning is a pro-life cause."

When we talk about voluntary family planning in the international context, what do we mean? The definition I use is enabling women and couples to determine the number of pregnancies and their timing, and equipping women to use voluntary methods for preventing pregnancy, not including abortion, that are harmonious with their values and beliefs.

It shocks Americans to learn that 1 in every 39 childbearing women in sub-Saharan Africa dies in childbirth. However, when a woman delays her first pregnancy until she is at least eighteen, her chances of surviving child-birth increase dramatically. If she can space her pregnancies—through fertility-awareness methods (sometimes called natural family planning) or modern contraceptive tools—to at least three years between births, she is more likely to survive and her children are more than twice as likely to survive infancy.

The Center for Strategic and International Studies (CSIS) hosted a delegation in February 2014 for congressional staff, foundation, and non-profit leaders, including Jenny Eaton Dyer, to see the emerging success of family planning in Ethiopia. With the infrastructure of their path-breaking Health Extension Worker (HEW) program, training 38,000 women as health workers in just a few years, women in the most rural communities now have access to antenatal care and family planning. With a Health Post designated for every 5,000 people, women have access to tools for healthy timing and spacing of pregnancies without having to walk for miles to a higher-level health facility. In less than a decade, since 2005, Ethiopia's contraceptive prevalence rate has nearly doubled, from 15 percent to 29 percent.

Healthy timing and spacing of pregnancies, alongside an increase in births taking place in Health Centers with skilled care during delivery and postpartum care, offers a strikingly successful model to reduce maternal mortality and improve child survival.

In addition to expanding access to voluntary family planning information and services, Melinda Gates, co-chair of the Bill & Melinda Gates Foundation, has also focused on healthy timing and spacing of pregnancies as a critical factor for global health and development. Hope Through Healing Hands, with support from the Gates Foundation, is promoting awareness and advocacy among Americans to support maternal, newborn, and child health. We are highlighting the crucial role that voluntary family planning is playing in nations such as Ethiopia.

Healthy timing and spacing of pregnancies does more than save lives from health risks: it also allows girls to stay in school. In Ethiopia, where the average age of marriage is just sixteen (with many girls married as young as age eleven), girls are often forced to drop out of secondary school to begin families. If girls can delay their first pregnancy and stay in school, ideally until the university level, they will be better equipped to partner with their husbands to meet their children's needs, in a more stable family economic environment.

And as First Lady Roman Tesfaye of Ethiopia stated, "When a mother can contribute to her own life and family, she contributes to the nation as a whole." Moving beyond the national level, healthy timing and spacing of pregnancies is also a key to other global health goals, like combating hunger and improving the status of women and girls. Family planning is a key, often hidden, engine for additional global health achievements.

Family Planning 2020 is a global partnership of more than 20 governments working with civil society, multilateral organizations, the private sector and others. Created at a 2012 London summit, it represents a commitment to meet the needs of an additional *120 million women* who want to delay or prevent pregnancy but lack access to information and tools.

With a focus on healthy timing and spacing of pregnancies, we can make major strides in just a few years. That's great news for mothers, children, and our entire world.

Bill Frist, MD, is a nationally acclaimed heart and lung transplant surgeon, former US Senate Majority Leader, and founder and chairman of Hope Through Healing Hands. Jenny Eaton Dyer, PhD, is the executive director of Hope Through Healing Hands. This article first appeared at TIME.com, March 21, 2014. Used by permission.

Chapter 3

Family Planning as a Pro-Life Cause

◄○► *Michael Gerson*

Visitors walking through the thatched houses of this village on the shore of Lake Kivu are shadowed by a large, happy rabble of young children. There are, however, few middle-aged women in evidence — perhaps not surprising in a country where a woman's average life expectancy is forty-nine.

After I talked to women in Bweremana, the correlation between the number of children and the absence of some of their mothers became clear. Kanyere Sabasaba, thirty-five, has had ten children, eight of whom have survived. Her last delivery did not go well. "I delivered the baby without any problem, but I was bleeding much," she told me. The case was too complex for the local health center, so Kanyere had to pay for her transport to another medical facility. After the surgery, the doctor performed a tubal ligation. "If I give birth again, I could die," she said. "The last child is the one who could really kill me."

In this part of Congo, the complications of childbirth are as dangerous as the militias in the countryside. One woman I met had given birth to thirteen children, only six of whom survived. Women sometimes deliver in the fields while working. Medical help can be a few days' journey away. Each birth raises the odds of a hemorrhage, infection, or rupture. Those odds increase dramatically when births come early in life, or late in life, or in rapid succession. In Congo, almost one in five deaths of women during childbearing years is due to maternal causes.

The women of Bweremana are attempting to diffuse and minimize their risk. In a program organized by Heal Africa, about 6,000 contribute the equivalent of 20 cents each Sunday to a common fund. When it is

33

their time to give birth, the fund becomes a loan to pay transportation and hospital fees. The women tend a common vegetable garden to help with income and nutrition. And the group encourages family planning.

The very words "family planning" light up the limbic centers of American politics. From a distance, it seems like a culture war showdown. Close up, in places such as Bweremana, family planning is undeniably pro-life. When births are spaced more than twenty-four months apart, both mothers and children are dramatically more likely to survive. Family planning results not only in fewer births, but in fewer at-risk births, including those early and late in a woman's fertility. When contraceptive prevalence is low, about 70 percent of all births involve serious risk. When prevalence is high, the figure is 35 percent.

Support for contraception does not imply or require support for abortion. Even in the most stringent Catholic teaching, the prevention of conception is not the moral equivalent of ending a life. And conservative Protestants have little standing to object to contraception, given the fact that they make liberal use of it. According to a 2009 Gallup poll, more than 90 percent of American evangelicals believe that hormonal and barrier methods of contraception are morally acceptable for adults. Children are gifts from God, but this does not require the collection of as many gifts as biologically possible.

> **The words "family planning" light up the limbic centers of American politics. From a distance, it seems like a culture war showdown. Close up, in places such as Bweremana, it is undeniably pro-life.**

Yet the role of contraception in development has become controversial — and both ideological extremes seem complicit in this polarization. Some liberal advocates of family planning believe that it is inseparable from abortion rights — while some conservative opponents of family planning believe exactly the same thing, leading them to distrust the entire enterprise. Suspicions on the right are not allayed when the vice president of the United States seems tolerant of forced abortion in China.

But women in Congo have enough home-grown problems without

importing irrelevant, Western controversies. While both the pill and condoms are generally available in larger cities such as Goma, access is limited in rural districts. Determining the pace of reproduction is often a male prerogative instead of a shared decision. Sexual violence can be as close for a woman as gathering fuel in the woods.

Contraceptives do not solve every problem. But women in Bweremana want access to voluntary family planning for the same reasons as women elsewhere: to avoid high-risk pregnancies, to deliver healthy children, and to better care for the children they have. And this is a pro-life cause.

Michael Gerson is an opinion writer for The Washington Post *and a former chief speechwriter for President George W. Bush. This article first appeared in* The Washington Post, *August 29, 2011 and was written in Bweremana, Democratic Republic of the Congo. Used by permission.*

Chapter 4

Transforming the World

◄○► *David Stevens*

I was wading through worms.

Cheplangat's bloated abdomen and recurrent vomiting masked the beauty of this eleven-year-old malnourished girl when I sleepily walked into the exam room of our small mission hospital in the "bush" of Kenya. I had walked a quarter of a mile up the hill from my house by flashlight, but her father had walked miles down rough Kenyan paths on a moonless night, carrying his seriously ill daughter to Tenwek Hospital's gate.

My exam revealed the obvious. Cheplangat had a bowel obstruction, and the X-ray hinted at the cause. It showed an all-too-common streaky mass. I rehydrated her, gave her a spinal block anesthetic, and then opened her abdomen to reveal the culprits.

Roundworms! Hundreds of roundworms in a big obstructing ball! I incised into Cheplangat's small intestine and pulled out half a dozen with a ringed forceps, putting them in a large metal basin by the operating table, where they wiggled and squirmed. Repeat! Repeat again, again, and again until the basin was almost full.

While I sutured her abdomen closed, I determined anew that something had to change. The problem was that her family didn't have a latrine, so parasite eggs were everywhere in the soil where the family defecated in the bushes around their hut. The worms had already caused her malnourishment and stunted growth.

As I pushed her gurney into the children's ward, I went by some of the 125 beds in our mission hospital, most containing two patients with multiple family caregivers sleeping on the floor. Three-fourths of our patients were women and children. Half of the hospital admissions and half of the deaths each year were from easily preventable diseases. How tragic!

I had felt God's call to be a missionary doctor in high school and had moved to Kenya with my wife and two children shortly after finishing my family practice residency. I was the third physician on staff, and we were the only hospital for over 300,000 people—an area equal to the population of Pittsburgh!

I had made rounds in this same ward earlier in the day. The child in the first bed was dehydrated from diarrhea and vomiting from drinking river water. The child lying beside her had severe malaria. In the next bed was a child who was septic from scabies, a skin parasite that covered almost his entire body with infected sores. The next child had rolled into the fire in the center of the hut while sleeping and had deep severe burns that would take multiple painful skin grafts over months.

While I was tucking in Cheplangat and writing some orders, the midwife found me and told me I urgently needed to see another patient in the delivery room. As I hurried over to that ward, I could hear brutal staccato coughing followed by a desperate gasp for breath from some of the many children in the whooping cough building. Another ward was full of kids with severe pneumonia from measles. A quarter of them would die despite our best efforts. Farther up the hill I could see the glow of a couple of lanterns through the windows of the tuberculosis ward. Those patients stayed for at least a month as they received daily injections and pills. How many of their family members had they infected at home before they came in?

The maternity ward was packed. Ninety percent of women delivered at home, but we got those with anticipated delivery problems—breech presentations, twins, and other issues. The overriding problem was the lack of child spacing. A woman didn't recover from one pregnancy before she had another. Children were often born premature, and they tended to be small, weak, and prone to diseases. Many didn't survive their first couple of years.

The problem tonight was that the baby was too big to go through the outlet of the mother's pelvis. In the United States we would have done a C-section, but this was her first baby and she would likely have ten or twelve more. With that many pregnancies, the C-section scar in her uterus might rupture, which would cause her to bleed to death. So putting her under local anesthesia, I did something we would never do in the United

States; I incised the ligament between her pubic bones to open her pelvis enough for a safe delivery, not only for this pregnancy, but also hopefully for those to come.

That night and others like it were the stimulus for a big idea. I could work sixteen-hour days every day for forever, but until we did something to prevent maternal-child diseases, the conveyor belt of suffering and death would never change. We treated children's dehydration, saved their lives, and then sent them home to drink the same contaminated water that got them sick in the first place. In a few months many would either die or be back in the hospital again, shriveled like a prune from dehydration.

But with only three physicians and six formally trained nurses, how could we do more? Without any form of mass communication, how could we change the health of people in our area whose lifestyles had been ingrained for hundreds of years?

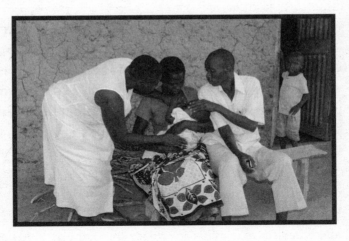

After prayer and lots of discussion, we decided to move one of our nurses into full-time maternal-children's health work in what we called Tenwek Community Health and Development. She would be the coordinator and I would be the director, adding those duties to my heavy hospital load. It was an inauspicious beginning, but I was determined to change the status quo. I could thwart more death and disease through prevention than I would ever cure at the hospital.

We realized we needed to design a scalable, low-cost approach that focused on community ownership of the program by using mainly volunteers. Three of the medicine dispensers we had informally trained became our supervisors. We then went out to three communities and sat down with leaders and started asking questions: "Do you have sickness here?" "What diseases do you see?" "Are women and children dying from them?"

As they recognized their problems, I then asked, "What are you willing to do about this?" The answer was always the same: "We can't do anything. You build us a clinic and pay for a nurse, and we will be healthy." I would reply, "I wish I could, but I don't have the money for a clinic or a nurse. What if you could do something with our help—would you do it?"

As they decided to "own" their problems, we asked them to select a dozen or so leaders from their community to form a Community Health Committee that we could train. The committee's first job after training was to identify seven volunteers who were willing to give three half days a week of their time as Community Health Helpers (CHHs) to the one hundred homes closest to theirs.

We needed to design a scalable, low-cost approach that focused on community ownership of the program by using mainly volunteers.

We intensely trained the first twenty-one volunteers from the first three villages over a four-week period. Half of the time was focused on learning psychosocial teaching methods for twenty-five health topics, using stories, songs, pictures, and dramas. That is how adults learn best. We taught them how to build a pit latrine, protect clean water sources, and build a raised fireplace to conserve firewood, prevent burns, and boil water for drinking.

They learned how to simply treat the ten most common diseases in our area, including malaria, dehydration, worms, headaches, peptic ulcer disease, first-aid issues, and more. They also learned how to do spiritual ministry in each home they visited. When asked how they got their "job," they would reply that they were volunteers. That always led to the question, "Why are you doing this then?" What an opportunity to share their motivation: Christ, who told them to love their neighbors!

We trained them to dispense family planning supplies, including birth control pills and condoms. Until that time in Kenya, you had to have a doctor or nurse dispense birth control pills, but women didn't want to stand in the family planning waiting line at the hospital for a day.

The bigger problem was that it was culturally unacceptable to limit the size of your family. The more children a woman had, the higher her status in the community. Once a woman had seven children, she was given the title *Chebuoset*, a term of great respect. I remember one very elderly man who brought his much younger wife to deliver at the hospital. When I asked how many children he had, he responded in the local Kipsigis language with great pride, "One hundred." I looked up from the chart I was writing on in disbelief. Further questioning revealed he had nine wives, and this one was the youngest with her first pregnancy!

Two things were the keys to our success in child spacing. First, we developed a ten-point screening questionnaire and proved to the government that when it was used by our CHHs, the complications from birth control pills were almost zero while frequent pregnancies had great risks for mother and baby.

We still had the cultural issue, which was a much harder nut to crack. A cultural issue needs a cultural solution, so we sat in lots of huts and drank lots of tea as we asked questions. We finally found the answer from an elder in the tribe. He shared that when polygamy was common, a man would not go sleep with his wife after she got pregnant until the top of her child's head was as high as his midthigh, which was usually around three years of age. My next question was the important one: "Were the women and their babies healthier then compared to now?"

He said, "Of course, but now few men can have more than one wife. It is just too expensive."

"What if there was an easy way for a man to still sleep with his wife but she wouldn't get pregnant until her child got to his midthigh?" I asked.

He stared into the fire for fifteen seconds, turned to me with a smile on his face, and said, *"Kararan!"* which literally means, "that would be beautiful." That became our cultural story to promote child spacing.

After training, we intensely motivated our volunteers. A supervisor made home visits with each CHH every month during their first year. They would observe the new CHH visiting a new home and document the family's health habits, which was the guide for what the CHH needed to teach. On every future visit, they would teach something the family needed to learn, show them how to dig a rubbish pit, or help them build a new latrine, dish drying rack, or raised fireplace. At the next house they visited, the supervisor would do the teaching so the CHH could learn from observing him. After each home visit, the two would sit down and discuss what happened.

Once a month, all seven CHHs would bring the women and children to a church, a school, or a meeting place under a tree where the children would be vaccinated. The supervisor could protect hundreds of children in a few hours with an air-powered immunization gun they had brought on the back of a motorcycle. They also met with the all the CHHs for continuing education at the monthly Community Health Committee meeting.

What set us apart and maximized our results was our use of nonfinancial incentives—instilling a sense of identity, ensuring great communication, enabling nonthreatening comparison, holding competitions, and encouraging a sense of family. We printed tables showing every CHH's accomplishments in a monthly newspaper that went out to every community. For example, we recognized the CHH who had the most home visits, the most new family planning users, and the committee whose CHHs had done the most. The health committees and CHHs were continually stimulated to do their work.

It was an intensive, time-consuming process, but we did another cycle every four months, training around eighty-five new volunteers each year. Within three years, we had 250 volunteers, each covering one hundred homes averaging seven people each, so we were in contact with more than half of the 300,000 people in our service area.

The results our survey data documented were amazing! Within five years, the percentage of homes with latrines quadrupled from 18 percent to 75 percent. The number of homes with clean water rose almost six-fold from 14 percent to 80 percent. The number of women spacing their children went up five-fold.

Our hospital data confirmed the impact of the program on patient morbidity and mortality. The isolation wards for whooping cough complications were often empty. We dropped from 106 cases annually to just three. Cases of dehydration from diarrhea and vomiting plummeted from 2,230 in the year we began to 403 just five years later. The number of tuberculosis patients getting treatment markedly increased initially as we found many undiagnosed cases and treated them, but then the numbers plunged.

A simple idea motivated the people to change their health habits. If a family changed five health habits—built and used a latrine, immunized their children, spaced their pregnancies, had a clean water source, and eliminated standing water sources where malaria-carrying mosquitoes bred—and this was documented with an inspection visit, the chief would call them to the front of the next *baraza*, an official meeting of the entire village. The chief would laud them before the crowd and then give them a beautiful "Healthy Home Certificate" with a gold seal and red ribbon on it. It is not *what* you give for an achievement, but *how* you give it! The significance, like at a university graduation, lay in who gave the recognition and that it was done in front of people they knew.

It is not *what* you give for an achievement, but *how* you give it!

The family would go home and put their certificate on the often bare wall of their hut, where it was an advertisement and motivator to anyone who entered their home. The first year, 150 families were awarded. By the fifth year of the program, more than 9,000 certificates were handed out. This motivator was so successful that we created another certificate for changing five more behaviors.

Maternal-child illnesses kill more women and children than any other disease, yet most of them are easily preventable. With volunteers, proven strategies, and motivational techniques, these problems can be addressed at low cost. I may have saved thousands of lives in our hospital using my medical training and surgical abilities, but I saved countless more lives through our community health efforts. It was so successful that we used the same methodology and started an economic development program that taught animal husbandry and agricultural techniques. Our spiritual ministry doubled the attendance and the number of churches in our service area.

Recently I traveled back to Kenya and visited Tenwek, which had developed into a 300-bed facility by the time I returned to the United States after eleven years of service. It is now a tertiary care center doing cardiac bypass surgery. The Community Health program now has more than 1,000 volunteers reaching more than 1 million people. The maternal-child issues we addressed are now solved, but in many places in the world, children and mothers still die by the millions.

If one part-time doctor and a nurse with limited funds can transform the health of so many people, what can all of us working together do to transform the world? More than you or I can imagine!

David Stevens, MD, MA (Ethics), is the CEO of Christian Medical and Dental Associations, the nation's largest faith-based organization of physicians and dentists. He spent thirteen years providing health care for women and children in Kenya, Sudan, and Somalia.

Chapter 5

The Burden We Should Share

◄o► *Cathy R. Taylor*

In developed countries, we have long known the "prescription" for a healthy baby — a baby born with the greatest chance to grow into a healthy, productive adult. The basic prescription is pretty simple. It starts with a healthy young woman, typically between the ages of twenty and thirty-five years old. She has at least a high school degree, and she has a supportive partner. She has access to health care, and the pregnancy is planned. The baby is wanted. If the couple has other children, eighteen to twenty-four months (but not more than five years) have lapsed since the woman's last delivery.

This is a simplified, basic accounting of the healthy mother and child "ingredients." Certainly there are others, yet if one of these is missing, the risk for a poor birth outcome increases. For instance, adolescent mothers are more likely to suffer from anemia and preeclampsia. Their babies are more likely to be born too small and too soon and to have developmental delays and disabilities. Pregnancy is particularly dangerous for very young girls (less than fifteen years old) who are emotionally and financially ill-equipped to care for a child; plus they are not physically developed enough to safely deliver an infant, thus stillbirth and birth traumas are more common.

Much of my career has been devoted to improving the health of young families in the southern United States, where birth outcomes are consistently worse than those reported for other states. Too many times I have seen the hardship that results from even a single unwanted pregnancy, yet in recent years our programs have targeted multiple missing healthy mother and child "ingredients." There is still much work to do (e.g., increasing rates of intended pregnancy and high school graduation, and providing full access to health care, etc.), but some critical indicators for maternal and child health have improved. It can be done.

Contrast this multifaceted approach, and the healthy mother and child prescription, with childbearing in developing countries where healthy ingredients are scant, a woman dies every two minutes from a pregnancy-related cause, and far more young girls and women suffer debilitating injuries that could be prevented. This tragic cycle is perpetuated by poverty, lack of education, prevalence of child marriage, and a lack of access to effective, affordable family planning and other health care services for women. In fact, the poorest, youngest, and most vulnerable children are most at risk, as globally more than 700 million women were married as children, some as young as nine years old. Once married, they are encouraged to become pregnant quickly, educational opportunities disappear, and their life choices grow limited.

Study after study links the education of women with their ability to avoid poverty, to lower their risk for premature illness and death, and to keep themselves and their children healthy. No matter the setting, promoting the health of young women, educating them, and allowing them to choose when they are spiritually, financially, and physically able to bear and care for a child will save lives and decrease the burden of loss and suffering.

Year after year, nurses are identified as the most trusted professionals by Gallup surveys, thus we are uniquely positioned to champion better health for at-risk women and their families. Teamed with our Allied Health colleagues and other professionals, we could challenge the devastating outcomes projected to be ahead for millions of women and children around the globe.

Christians are called to carry each other's burdens in order to fulfill the law of Christ (Galatians 6:2). We have the prescription and the means. This is a burden we should share.

Cathy R. Taylor, DrPH, MSN, RN, is dean and professor at Gordon E. Inman College of Health Sciences and Nursing at Belmont University in Nashville, Tennessee.

Chapter 6

Baby Free Until 2013

◄◌► James and Jena Lee Nardella

When we married in December 2007, we wanted time to build our marriage and our careers before having children. So we concocted a whimsical battle cry: "Baby Free Until 2013!" We would repeat this with a wry smile each time friends and family asked about our child-rearing plans. In the summer of 2013, after thoughtful conversations, we decided to go off birth control. And lo and behold, before we could count the days in a month, we were pregnant. The battle cry worked.

As we watched Jena's belly grow each month, we realized how fortunate we were, especially as some of our closest friends and family have not had nearly as much ease conceiving. We also recognized that thousands of adolescent girls in Africa do not have the choice to delay parenthood or even marriage.

You see, we work for two organizations that provide health care to HIV-infected and affected persons in Africa, and we have been given a unique window into the lives of young women in Kenya, Uganda, Zambia, Ethiopia, Rwanda, and Central African Republic. For our young female friends in this part of the world, the nuanced discussion of timing and spacing of babies is very different from the one we hear in the United States.

In Lwala, Kenya, where our work overlaps, 16 to 20 percent of the adult population is HIV positive. The Lwala Community Hospital is providing more than one thousand of these HIV patients with lifesaving medical care. The effects have been remarkable, with hope and health returning to a place where average life expectancy had dropped to forty years of age. However, the progress overlooks a worrying trend: the HIV epidemic is disproportionately affecting adolescent girls and young mothers. In Lwala, females make up 94.8 percent of HIV-positive clients in the fifteen-to-twenty-four age group. In 2013 more than 300 girls under the age of eighteen had babies, representing about 15 percent of the adolescent female population. Through our mentorship program, we support a group of fifty-eight girls who are middle school dropouts and were saddened to realize that more than 80 percent of those girls are already mothers. These statistics are not abstract when you really know these girls and their circumstances.

Try to imagine life through the eyes of our friend Sarah, who is just fourteen years old and a new mother to a premature baby boy named Moses. Sarah did not plan on getting pregnant, but during her Christmas break from school, an older neighbor forced himself on her while he was drunk. (Her circumstance now makes her part of a national trend in Kenya, where three out of ten girls report having experienced sexual violence before age eighteen.) While her parents know about the rape, they have decided not to confront the neighbor but, instead, are pressuring Sarah to marry her perpetrator.

When Sarah brought baby Moses to the hospital for immunizations, she asked the nurse for birth control pills to delay any future pregnancy, but the nurse told her they were not available without parental permission. Sarah's mind raced with questions: *How do I avoid getting pregnant again? How can I protect myself if my parents will not protect me? How will I return to school?*

For many of us, as Americans, Sarah's scenario may seem like an unimaginable predicament related to teenagers, sexual abuse, pregnancy, and contraception. However, data from the Lwala Community Hospital reveal a nearly 60 percent spike in teen deliveries forty weeks out from each school holiday, pointing to a window of sexual vulnerability for adolescents during each break. Teens are vulnerable to unplanned pregnancies — and thus unprotected sex and exposure to HIV and other sexually transmitted infections — during these month-long breaks.

Something must be done to protect girls in Lwala and other rural places — and it can be done. Kenyan churches can help by holding men accountable, by hosting school-break camps in their local areas, and by providing safe spaces for teenage girls and boys to talk about the risks they may face. Local health care providers can help by providing youth-friendly access to contraceptive choices so that the Sarahs of this world do not face catch-22s with life-altering consequences. American Christians can help by having the courage to participate in the conversation and by being open to the range of moral and medical responses to the challenge. Our government and other international players can help by taking a larger stake in achieving universal access to voluntary family planning and responsible education for young people in hard-to-reach places.

As Christians, the two of us are propelled by our faith in a loving and merciful God to do the work we do in Africa. A majority of the year, we make our home in Tennessee, a solidly red state. We are neither abortion rights activists nor "lefty liberals." However, we do want teenagers in Africa to have greater access to contraception for protection from unplanned pregnancies and HIV.

We understand why some people of faith in America are hesitant to support increased access to contraceptive choices, especially for young people. But because of our time spent in rural African communities and because of the girls we know, such as Sarah, our view has broadened. The nuanced circumstances of young mothers cannot be addressed with one-dimensional responses. Simple black-and-white reactions do not seriously consider the complexity and urgency of the dilemma for many vulnerable girls around the world. International policies, politics, and financing must do more to account for the real predicaments adolescents face.

We believe young women should have the right to time their child rearing, to protect themselves against HIV, and to pursue healthy productive lives. We believe teenage girls should be able to avoid unintended pregnancies and the difficult decisions and desperate measures that often follow. We believe contraceptive access and choice are important in the fight against poverty and HIV. As we welcome our own baby into the world, we invite you to join us in respectfully broadening the conversation around contraception to include the perspective and urgency of our teenage friends in Africa.

James Nardella is the executive director of the Lwala Community Alliance, a development project in Lwala, Kenya. Jena Lee Nardella is the co-founder of Blood:Water Mission. The two have a son and split their time between Nashville, Tennessee, and their mutual work in East Africa.

Chapter 7

Women and Girls' Health

It's More Than Maternal Mortality

◄○► *Phillip Nieburg*

During a recent trip to Tanzania, I had the opportunity to reflect on broader women's health issues in a way that I hadn't done before. To cut to the chase, there is no doubt that in developing countries, high maternal mortality rates, reflecting the large numbers of deaths of women during or just after pregnancy, is a terrible problem that deserves more attention and resources. Many—if not most—of the nearly 300,000 maternal deaths that occur every year could be avoided if women in those countries had the same kind of access to emergency care and access to contraception that women in the United States and other industrialized countries take for granted. Based in part on what I saw in Tanzania, I recently wrote the report "Improving Maternal Mortality and Other Aspects of Women's Health: The United States' Global Role," which addresses key challenges to improving maternal mortality and women's health worldwide and talks about what the related priorities of US foreign policy should be.

The tragedy of maternal mortality deserves all the attention it currently gets—and much more. But it would be a mistake to think of women's poor pregnancy outcomes as an isolated set of purely medical challenges that can be solved by a narrow focus on emergency care.

First, some pregnancy-related deaths are not included in the current definition of maternal mortality. For example, recent research indicates that women who survive difficult labors and deliveries have a mortality risk six times higher than the risk faced by women whose pregnancy was normal. This excess mortality risk lasts as long as four years after the high-risk delivery. However, the currently accepted definition of maternal mortality does not include maternal deaths that occur more than forty-two days after delivery. (An extended definition of the maternal period to include the first twelve months after delivery has been proposed but has not yet come into widespread use.) Another source of undercounting of pregnancy deaths is the specific exclusion of homicide and suicide as causes of maternal deaths. Although there is strong evidence that pregnant women in many countries are at increased risk of homicide—and suggestive evidence for risk of suicide—neither of these causes are included specifically in the current definition of maternal mortality, which excludes deaths "... from accidental or incidental injuries."

It is also clear that death of pregnant women is not the only severe maternal outcome of pregnancy. For every woman who dies because of events related to a pregnancy, there are anywhere from fifteen to thirty other women who survive pregnancy, but suffer one or more long-term or permanent pregnancy-related physical or social disabilities, including— but not limited to—infertility, prolapsed uterus, severe nutritional deficiencies, severe postpartum depression, or other long-term challenges. For example, one of the worst consequences of a prolonged or "obstructed" labor at the end of an otherwise normal pregnancy is development of an obstetric fistula, caused by the intense pressures on maternal organs generated by the muscles of the uterus as prolonged efforts to expel the baby fail. As a consequence of the resulting leakage of urine or feces, women with obstetric fistulas often suffer from social exclusion, chronic urinary or fecal incontinence, and other health problems. The World Health Organization estimates that as many as 2 million women, mostly in sub-Saharan Africa and South Asia, are now living with untreated obstetric fistulas, with 50,000 to 100,000 more women added to the toll each year. It is particularly tragic that prolonged or obstructed labor occurs most often in younger adolescents, because their pelvic structures are not yet mature.

Because of the clear association between unplanned pregnancies and maternal mortality, decreasing unplanned pregnancies through various means (e.g., addressing the unmet need for family planning, reducing sexual violence, reducing numbers of child marriages) would help reduce numbers of both maternal deaths and the nonfatal but severe adverse maternal outcomes of pregnancy noted earlier. In fact, a recent detailed study of information from 167 countries found that just addressing the unmet need for family planning in those countries would reduce maternal mortality by 29 percent. Presumably, the nonfatal but severe outcomes would be reduced to a similar degree.

Also, some women in their childbearing years are unable to have children; others choose not to become pregnant. In addition, aging populations in most countries include growing numbers of postmenopausal women. For these groups and for other women, a number of important health challenges remain that are not directly related to pregnancy. For example, the prevention, early detection, and adequate treatment of cervical cancer, breast cancer, and sexually transmitted infections are each ongoing challenges to women's health in all countries.

Rather than continuing what appears to me as a piecemeal approach to global aspects of reproductive health, with separate programs to address (e.g., gender-based violence, women and HIV/AIDS, maternal mortality, family planning, cervical cancer, girls' education), I argue in my report that the United States should develop and implement a comprehensive global plan for women's health that includes males as well as females, using coordinated prevention and care programming for each stage of the reproductive health life cycle.

Phillip Nieburg is a senior associate at the Global Health Policy Center of the Center for Strategic and International Studies. This article first appeared at SmartGlobalHealth .org, October 25, 2012. Used by permission.

Chapter 8

She Counts

<o> *Shannon Trilli*

We can't forget her. We can't forget any of them: the expectant mothers in still-developing nations who hope against long odds to make it through their pregnancies and safely deliver healthy babies. Despite global strides in improving maternal health, the journey of these women remains treacherous. Last July, I got an up-close look.

I was on a site visit at Nyadire Hospital, a United Methodist mission hospital in Zimbabwe. Dr. Tshiani Kasongo is the lead doctor and surgeon there. My colleagues and I had arrived dusty and weary after a long drive from the capital and were welcomed at the Nyadire Mission guest house by some excited volunteers from the United States.

Ahead of us, a pregnant woman also had arrived at the hospital, and Dr. Kasongo had invited one of the teenage volunteers, who aspired to become a doctor, to observe the emergency C-section. The young volunteer returned later that night, elated to have seen twins delivered.

The next day, during a routine tour of the hospital, I congratulated Dr. Kasongo on the successful delivery. But he shook his head and quietly reported that the mother did not survive. His solemnity was in stark contrast to the exuberance of the volunteer who had witnessed the surgery. Clearly, she had not understood that the twins had come into this world as orphans.

What happened?

Dr. Kasongo explained that he had received an emergency call that morning: a woman in an outlying area had been in labor for two days. Her family belonged to a Christian denomination that doesn't believe in the use of modern medicine or doctors. Although her labor was clearly abnormal, she was not permitted to seek help.

She grew weaker and weaker. Finally, over the objections of the men in the home, the woman's mother called for an ambulance. But the local vehicle had no fuel. The family scrambled to find or borrow money to gas up the ambulance. It took them all day to unite enough cash to buy the fuel and then make the long journey over rough roads to Nyadire Hospital.

By the time they reached Dr. Kasongo, he knew it was probably too late for the mother — and he suspected the distress of prolonged labor may also have been too traumatic for the babies inside her womb. He told me later that when he made the initial incision, the mother's blood was so thin from fighting the labor for three days that she just bled and bled. There were no nutrients left in her exhausted body.

But the twins were alive, and Dr. Kasongo delivered two healthy baby girls. The grandmother, who would likely now become a mother again and raise them, had just left the hospital before our morning tour began.

How *unnecessary* this young mother's death was! And yet her case is not unique; she represents *hundreds of thousands of women* around the world who die every year — one every two minutes — from complications during pregnancy or childbirth.

> **Why have we as a global community not crossed the finish line of reducing maternal deaths by 75 percent?**

According to the latest United Nations report, improving maternal health is one of the Millennium Development Goals (MDGs) that continue to lag behind expectations. Our understanding of the correct interventions, targets, and messages to prevent maternal mortality has grown in recent decades, and maternal deaths have declined by 47 percent since the MDGs were announced. So, why have we as a global community not crossed the finish line of reducing maternal deaths by 75 percent?

There is no single reason for this — only the sum of many preventable reasons: incomprehension, especially among men, of family planning (FP) and of the antenatal and delivery needs of pregnant women; societal biases that affect women; a dearth of surgeons in hospitals and of midwives in local clinics; inadequate roads and transportation from remote rural settings to medical facilities; and the lack of financial resources — poverty — to name a few.

At Nyadire Hospital, Dr. Kasongo is confronting these issues by promoting community health education, sending general nurses for midwifery training, recruiting qualified staff to strengthen the hospital's mother-and-child health program, encouraging in-hospital deliveries, and improving the availability of resources such as medicine, transportation, and medical equipment. United Methodists, as communities of faith in Zimbabwe and around the globe, are using the pulpit to talk about and change attitudes and behaviors that contribute to maternal mortality.

These measures are helping to dramatically reduce maternal deaths in Nyadire. Surely, with a concerted effort and adequate funding, these measures and more can be promoted and replicated around the globe to improve the fate of mothers and their children, and we can reach our goal by 2015.

"We can end preventable child and maternal deaths," UNICEF head, Anthony Lake, said recently, "and if we don't, shame on us. History will judge us harshly — as well it should."

Shannon Trilli is the director of the Global Health Initiative for the United Methodist Committee on Relief.

Chapter 9

New Ideas, New Opinions

How Fertility Awareness-based Methods Are Saving Women's Lives Worldwide

◄○► *Victoria Jennings*

Mothers and children around the world face danger every day.

Healthy mothers and children are the foundation for strong families and, ultimately, strong communities. The health of a mother and the health of her children are intricately linked, and the greatest health risks for both occur during pregnancy, childbirth, and the postpartum period. Research reveals that every day approximately 800 women die from pregnancy-related complications and 99 percent of those women live in developing countries.[1] In addition, for every woman who dies of pregnancy-related causes, twenty to thirty survivors suffer serious pregnancy-related illness and disability.[2]

Pregnancy is the leading cause of death for young women ages fifteen to nineteen worldwide. Early childbearing is particularly common in South Asia and sub-Saharan Africa. In fact, almost all adolescent births—about 95 percent—occur in low- and middle-income countries where girls are physically immature and undernourished, increasing the risk of obstetric complications and death. In the poorest regions of the world, over one in three girls has given birth by the age of eighteen.[3]

Furthermore, the risk of death increases dramatically for children whose mothers die in childbirth.[4] The mortality rates are also higher for infants born to very young mothers as they are more likely to be premature,

1. World Health Organization, "Maternal Mortality," *Fact Sheet,* no. 348 (May 2014), http://www.who.int/mediacentre/factsheets/fs348/en/.

2. Tabassum Firoz a, Doris Chou b, Peter von Dadelszen a, Priya Agrawal c, Rachel Vanderkruik d, Ozge Tunçalp b, Laura A Magee a, Nynke van Den Broek e, Lale Say b, for the Maternal Morbidity Working Group. "Measuring Maternal Health: Focus on Maternal Morbidity," *Bulletin of the World Health Organization* (2013); 91:794–96.

3. World Health Organization, "Adolescent Pregnancy," *Fact Sheet,* no. 364 (September 2014), http://www.who.int/mediacentre/factsheets/fs364/en/.

4. Joanne Katz, Keith P. West Jr., Subarna K. Khatry, Parul Christian, Steven C. LeClerq et al., "Risk

have low birth weights, and suffer from complications of delivery.[5] Close spacing of births increases the risks: Babies born less than two years after a sibling are more than twice as likely to die in the first year of life compared to those born three years after a sibling.[6]

Can family planning save lives? Yes.

Studies have shown that allowing women and couples to delay their first birth and space subsequent pregnancies three to five years apart has dramatic effects on the health of the children and the mother, thereby improving the health and well-being of the whole family and the community.

Experts estimate that the use of family planning to space births coupled with adequate pregnancy care could prevent nearly half of newborn deaths and two-thirds of maternal deaths in the developing world.[7] The use of family planning for healthy timing and spacing of pregnancies can dramatically improve the health and survival of both women and children. By preventing unintended pregnancies, family planning could also prevent 25 million induced abortions and reduce the number of deaths due to unsafe abortion by 80 percent.[8]

Of the 208 million pregnancies that occur each year, 40 percent are unintended.[9] This is because more than 222 million women and their partners around the world who would like to avoid pregnancy are not currently using a method of family planning.[10] There are many reasons why these women

Factors for Early Infant Mortality in Sarlahi District, Nepal." *Bulletin of the World Health Organization* 81 (November 25, 2003): 717–25.

Ronsmans C, Chowdhury ME, Dasgupta SK, Ahmed A, Kaoblinsky M. (2010) "Effect of parent's death on child survival in rural Bangladesh: a cohort study." *Lancet* 375: 2024–2031.

Masmas TN, Jensen H, da Silva D, Hoj L, Sandstrom A, et al. (2004) "Survival among motherless children in rural and urban areas in Guinea-Bissau." *Acta Paediatr* 93: 99–105.

Anderson FWJ, Morton SU, Naik S, Gebrian B. (2007) "Maternal mortality and the consequences on infant and child survival in rural Haiti." *Maternal Child Health Journal* 11: 395–401.

5. Rhonda Smith, Lori Ashford, James Gribble, and Donna Clifton. "Family Planning Saves Lives." Population Reference Bureau. 2009.

6. Shea O. Rutstein, "Effects of Preceding Birth Intervals on Neonatal, Infant and Under-Five Years Mortality and Nutritional Status in Developing Countries: Evidence From the Demographic and Health Surveys," *International Journal of Gynecology and Obstetrics* 89 (2005): S7-24.

7. Guttmacher Institute, "Facts on investing in family planning and maternal and newborn health," *In Brief,* New York: Guttmacher Institute, 2010.

8. Ibid.

9. Singh S, Sedgh G, and Hussain R, "Unintended pregnancy: worldwide levels, trends, and outcomes," *Studies in Family Planning,* 2010, 41(4):241–250.

10. Susheela Singh et al., "Adding it Up: The Costs and Benefits of Investing in Family Planning

do not use family planning. Services and supplies may not be available. Some may have used family planning but dropped out because they were not properly prepared for possible side effects, could not find a method suited to their particular needs, or ran out of supplies.[11] Individuals may fear partner opposition or social disapproval, and others simply lack knowledge about method options and their use. Among these, the most frequently cited reasons for women not using a method of family planning are fear of side effects or health concerns, infrequent intercourse (most often due to partner migrating for work), perceived opposition, and postpartum amenorrhea or breast-feeding.[12]

These obstacles can be overcome by providing a full range of method options, training health providers to deliver comprehensive information and counseling, expanding the reach of family planning services, increasing fertility awareness,[13] and improving gender equality and shared decision-making between men and women.

Fertility awareness-based methods, an evidence-based solution offering new possibilities

Fertility awareness-based methods (FAM) can address the principal obstacles to family planning use. FAMs are modern and effective methods based on reproductive physiology and work by identifying the fertile days of a woman's menstrual cycle. To prevent pregnancy, couples abstain or use a barrier method during the fertile days.

Given their ease of use and lack of side effects, FAMs may appeal

---

and Maternal and Newborn Health" (New York: Guttmacher Institute and UNFPA, 2009), http://www.guttmacher.org/pubs/AddingItUp2009.pdf.

11. John Bongaarts, Judith Bruce, "The Causes of Unmet Need for Contraception and the Social Content of Services," *Studies in Family Planning* 26, no. 2 (March–April 1995): 57–75; Assefa Hailemariam, Fikrewold Haddis, "Factors Affecting Unmet Need for Family Planning in Southern Nations, Nationalities and Peoples Region, Ethiopia," *Studies in Family Planning* 28, no. 3 (September 1997): 173–91; Charles F. Westoff, Akinrinola Bankole, "Unmet Need: 1990–1994," *Demographic and Health Surveys Comparative Studies* 16 (June 1995), http://dhsprogram.com/pubs/pdf/CS16/00FrontMatter00.pdf.

12. Gilda Sedgh, Rubina Hussain, "Reasons for Contraceptive Nonuse among Women Having Unmet Need for Contraception in Developing Countries," *Studies in Family Planning* 45, no. 2 (June 2014), https://www.guttmacher.org/pubs/journals/j.1728-4465.2014.00382.x.pdf.

13. Fertility Awareness is actionable information about fertility throughout the life cycle and the ability to apply this knowledge to one's own circumstances and needs. Specifically, it includes basic information about the menstrual cycle, when and how pregnancy occurs, the likelihood of pregnancy from unprotected intercourse at different times during the cycle and at different life stages, and the role of male fertility. Fertility Awareness can also include information on how specific family planning methods work, how they affect fertility, and how to use them; and it can create the basis for understanding, communicating about, and correctly using family planning.

to couples who are not currently using any method, those relying on a traditional method, or those who are dissatisfied with their current or past method. FAMs can empower women by helping them understand their bodies and accurately predict their likelihood of pregnancy. FAMs resonate with communities because they are natural and directly linked to fertility concepts, which are strong cultural forces in many societies. Traditional guardians of community norms, including religious leaders, have welcomed FAMs as consistent with their social norms and values. Therefore, FAMs are an important addition to the method mix that could help many couples prevent unplanned pregnancies.

The Institute for Reproductive Health at Georgetown University has developed three easy-to-teach and use methods that are being integrated into family planning programs around the world.

Standard Days Method® (SDM) identifies a fixed set of days during each menstrual cycle when a woman can get pregnant if she has unprotected intercourse. If the woman does not want to get pregnant, she and her partner avoid unprotected intercourse on days eight through nineteen of her cycle. A woman can use CycleBeads®, a color-coded string of beads, to help track the days of her menstrual cycle and see which days she is most likely to get pregnant.

TwoDay Method® is a fertility awareness method of family planning that uses cervical secretions to indicate fertility. A woman using the TwoDay Method checks for cervical secretions at least twice a day. If she notices secretions of any type, color, or consistency either "today" or "yesterday," she considers herself fertile.

Lactational Amenorrhea Method (LAM) is a short-term family planning method based on the natural effect of breastfeeding on fertility. The act of breastfeeding, particularly exclusive breastfeeding, suppresses the release of hormones that are necessary for ovulation. If the following conditions are met, the method provides protection from pregnancy:
1. Mother's monthly bleeding has not returned since her baby was born, AND
2. The baby is only/exclusively breastfed (day and night), AND
3. The baby is less than six months old.

Though included in many program guidelines, FAMs are frequently not offered because of provider bias and insufficient knowledge.[14] Because

---

14. Suyapa Pavon, Claudia Velasquez, Rebecka Lundgren, "Informed Choice in Natural Methods in Family Planning Programs, Final Report," *Tegucigalpa* (2003).

FAMs represent a type of method different from the hormonal and barrier methods that programs typically offer, they have the potential to reach a different segment of the population, including men.

The responsibility of planning one's family belongs to both women and men. Thus, it is important that men are educated about reproductive health and the options available for delaying and spacing births. One of the defining attributes of FAM is that men must be involved. Successful use of these methods depends on the man's cooperation in avoiding unprotected sex on fertile days. Research indicates that men often care about women's health and want to be involved in family planning. However, many programs place little emphasis on men. FAM encourages programs to view family planning as more than a woman's responsibility and to consider the role that men could play in the couple's family planning choice. Therefore, incorporation of FAM into programs is likely to contribute to increased male involvement in a range of reproductive health decisions.

What do users say about the effects of FAM use on their lives?

Most users report enhanced feelings of love, mutual respect, control of their fertility, and physical well-being. In rural India, more than 90 percent of women using SDM reported increased communication, affection, understanding, and improved ability to discuss sex.[15] Results from in-depth interviews with SDM users suggested that the experience of using SDM was empowering for many women. Women were able to understand the menstrual cycle and how the method worked to prevent pregnancy. In a study conducted in Guatemala, women reported a significant increase in the ability to care for their health, refuse sex, and communicate with their partners after six months of SDM use.[16]

"The SDM has helped us to become closer, understand each other's needs. Unlike earlier, we now discuss intimate things with each other,

---

15. Loveleen Johri, D.S. Panwar, Rebecka Lundgren, "Introduction of the Standard Days Method in CARE-India's Community-Based Reproductive Health Programs," The Institute for Reproductive Health Georgetown University for the U.S. Agency for International Development (USAID) (October 2005), http://irh.org/wp-content/uploads/2013/05/PNADG769.pdf.

16. "Comparison of Standard Days Method® User Tools," Institute for Reproductive Health, Georgetown University for the U.S. Agency for International Development (USAID) (February 2008), http://pdf.usaid.gov/pdf_docs/PNADL888.pdf.

and this has added pleasure to our otherwise monotonous sex life."
—Male SDM user, India

"I feel good that my husband now understands how my body works. He pays attention to my suggestions and respects my wishes. For the first time he asks me if we can have intercourse. I am happy that he cares about me."—Female SDM user, India

"Knowledge of the safe and unsafe periods has been liberating."
—Female SDM user, El Salvador

"Ever since using SDM I have noticed many positive changes for myself and my relationship. I have a better understanding of the way my body works, including fertile and infertile days, something I never thought about before. SDM is a very discreet method. It provides great autonomy in the way we manage our relationship. It does not require any resupply from the health agent or any follow-up appointment at the health center. Physical sex with my husband has become more harmonious. SDM has breathed new life into our relationship."—Female SDM user, Mali

New ideas like FAM have been shown to fill a gap in needed health services for the many women who currently are at risk of unintended pregnancy. These are methods that teach women about their bodies and empower them to discuss sensitive topics with their male partners. Providing these methods to women who can and want to use them fits well with philosophies of strengthening families and honoring human dignity.

Now is a critical time for donors, governments, health professionals, and nongovernmental organizations (NGOs) to join together in addressing the family planning needs of women and couples around the world. Global poverty and its consequences, like maternal and newborn deaths, are one of the greatest challenges of our generation. Through collaboration, commitment, open-mindedness, and innovation, they can be overcome.

––––––––––––

Victoria Jennings, PhD, is the director and principal investigator of the Institute for Reproductive Health, as well as a professor of the Department of Obstetrics and Gynecology at Georgetown University.

Chapter 10

Who Will Take Care of My Children?

◄o► *Elizabeth Styffe*

When I watch mourners in Kenya, Malawi, Uganda, and many other countries walk down the road behind the wooden casket of a mother and child held high on the shoulders of men in the village, I am reminded again, *This is not a cause. This is an emergency.*

Pregnant women all over the developing world ask two tragic questions: "Am I going to die?" and "Who will take care of my children?"

How can women be asking these questions when they are young and full of life?

There is a compassionate mandate for mothers to live and for children to survive—and thrive—in the arms of their mother. One can judge the morality of a country by the way it cares for its women and children. If ever there was something worth fighting for, keeping mothers and babies alive and together tops them all. But—

The statistics of maternal and infant death are gut-wrenching, vivid, and real. One in thirty-nine women in sub-Saharan Africa are dying during pregnancy or childbirth. There is a moral mandate to provide accurate information and the resources necessary for life while honoring a woman and family's cultural and faith values. Through no fault of their own, 222 million women have limited ability to influence the timing or spacing of their pregnancies, leaving these women and their children vulnerable.

When a woman's cries and wailings are heard, the numbers stop being just statistics and become the stories of real people. Numbers are numbing. As one Rwandan woman told me, "Numbers are statistics. Numbers are statistics with the tears wiped off."

But there is hope, and the answer is to keep mothers alive by equipping them to have pregnancies timed and spaced in ways that promote health, including prenatal care, a skilled attendant at birth, and a host of other supportive interventions, so that the mothers and fathers can care for their children. Because every child deserves a family.

But how?

The keys to information and transformation lie in a frequently overlooked source. For families to receive what they need, they can go to the church, which becomes an outpost not just for spiritual health, but for physical health as well.

Recently, I was working in Rwanda alongside Juliette, a health volunteer who trains church members to, in turn, become trainers volunteering in their communities. Although from different parts of the globe, Juliette and I both are part of the PEACE Plan movement, an initiative of Saddleback Church of Lake Forest, California, where Pastor Rick Warren has launched 20,000 ordinary members of the church to travel globally. To do this, he has empowered and linked churches in 197 countries. Using a train-the-trainer approach, the PEACE Plan has equipped more than 500,000 ordinary people in church pews — or wooden benches — at the most grassroots levels to identify, prioritize, and act on problems in their own communities through the local churches.

Juliette, along with another trainer, simply walks to seven homes — some of them up to an hour away — to talk to women about pregnancy, about the value of timing and spacing pregnancy, directing them to tools that are in keeping with their Christian faith.

When Juliette ducks through the piece of fabric that hangs at the front door of each home she visits, she is comfortable and credible. Armed with a teaching plan and genuine compassion for her neighbors, she listens and teaches basic hygiene principles, HIV prevention, and healthy pregnancy.

Volunteering four hours a week, Juliette has reduced the maternal mortality rate in her neighborhood. She is an expert, even though her formal education ended before the fifth grade. Early on, Juliette taught me about dying mothers, dying babies, and the indescribable pain of both. I always listen when she speaks. She proves that when the church is involved, information is accessible to the local community. The church is indispensable in terms of access to health care training and in terms of reliability and accuracy of message.

Juliette had my attention when she said, "Maybe one of the reasons we don't name our babies for one month after birth is that we're not sure they will survive." Juliette spoke stoically, as if her storehouse of tears had been emptied at the graves of too many. I swallowed hard. She continued to teach from a well-crafted lesson plan that was both accurate and personal.

"Our bodies are tired and weak. Today we will be talking about pregnancy and how to get healthy before getting pregnant and how to make sure our bodies are ready so that our babies can survive." The lesson plan was clear, and fifty trainers — both women and their husbands — had come to hear it.

"There are medicines and methods to help you. We must be more intentional in preparing our bodies for our babies, for their sake and for ours. I am a Christian, and I use pills to help me. There is nothing wrong with using techniques or tools. I'm not interfering with God's will if I take medicine. When there is information and resources for timing and spacing of pregnancies and I withhold it because I am afraid of offending others, I am telling people they can die."

> **"Maybe one of the reasons we don't name our babies for one month after birth is that we're not sure they will survive."**

Then Juliette taught the class a biblical principle that is empowering and life-changing. She spoke about stewardship. "Every gift we have comes from God. God also gave me ways to be pregnant. He gave me eggs, and I'm responsible for them."

The idea of stewardship — of being accountable to God for the gifts he has given me and seeing scientific knowledge as a gift he has given to influence my life practices — is not new. All truth is God's truth.

This is the type of training that equips laypeople to deliver the message in churches all over the world. At least two things stand in the way of helping women and children survive and thrive through healthy timing and spacing of children, yet there is a solution that is underused and fully available everywhere. Every woman and family needs this: Accurate knowledge and resources that honor a woman and family's cultural and biblical values, and a distribution channel that is accessible and trusted to deliver the information and resources.

One of the reasons women do not have what they need is that they can't access it. I have seen villages where there is no post office, school, or hospital, but there is a church. And this is the hope. Churches can provide accurate information closest to the people who need it.

Alongside the suffering, there are churches filled with people who are willing and able to make a difference. There is a group of people in the faith community that can tackle any problem at a grassroots level. Mobilizing ordinary members in churches everywhere to train others brings information, tools, and hope. Referrals are made to tertiary settings when the challenges are complex. For timing and spacing of pregnancies, church-based grassroots education and interventions launch an idea to scale-up possibilities. Life and mind-set change rarely happens in a government office, but it can happen in a church.

The church is the greatest untapped source of information and hope in the twenty-first century. And today 4,800 Rwandan trainers teaching church-based classes and making home visits in Rwanda provide proof that the church is a distribution giant ready to serve.

Churches are located in communities where women and children are needlessly dying. Churches are a trusted source of information. Churches are accessible, available, and influential in communities. It's time to look to the church for help in solving the problems of maternal and child health.

Elizabeth Styffe, RN, MN, PHN, is the global director for HIV&AIDS and Orphan Care Initiatives at Saddleback Church in Lake Forest, California. She and her husband have seven children, including three adopted from Rwanda.

Chapter 11

A "Big Tent" Approach

Healthy Timing and Spacing of Pregnancy

≺o≻ *Kent R. Hill*

World Vision is pro-life and strongly supports healthy timing and spacing of pregnancies (HTSP). Let me tell you why.

World Vision supports the first 1,000 days of a child's life, in collaboration with a US government initiative. The 1,000 days between a child's conception and his or her second birthday offer a unique window of opportunity to shape healthier and more prosperous futures. The right nutrition during this 1,000-day window can have a profound impact on the mother's health and her child's ability to grow and learn, thus helping to enable families, communities, and countries to break the cycle of poverty.

During the same 1,000-day window, HTSP provides a child the opportunity to obtain proper nutrition while allowing the mother to replenish nutrients lost during pregnancy and breastfeeding.

In my experience, though family planning (FP) is primarily viewed through the prism of women's health, research has shown that women themselves view family planning in broader terms. They believe that having smaller families and spacing births can both improve health and increase opportunities for education. But even larger families benefit from HTSP and can enable better educational opportunities for children, thus helping to achieve important development goals.

To be an effective faith-based coalition with a goal of providing information and services on HTSP and family planning, it is important to keep in mind the cultural and religious sensitivities in the countries in which we work. This is true in the United States, and it is true abroad. A diversity of family planning options, including natural family planning, for example, shows respect and sensitivity for women, their spouses, and the cultural and religious contexts in which the women live.

In the interests of both mothers and children, it is imperative that a "big tent" approach be taken toward family planning. A key component of such an approach that all can agree on is HTSP.

We, along with development partners, have witnessed a drop in the estimated annual number of under-five deaths from 12.6 million in 1990 to 6.6 million in 2012,[1] mostly due to child survival strategies. Many such deaths, however, can still be reduced by expanding access to family planning. Births that are spaced too close together, too early, or too late in a woman's life decrease both the mother's and infant's chances for survival. Children born too close together face increased risk of contracting and dying from infectious diseases and can suffer high rates of malnutrition. By helping women space births at least three years apart and bear children during their healthiest years, family planning could prevent many of these deaths.

People like me who are committed to decreasing maternal and child deaths need to understand that it is imperative that we work together with a variety of options and opinions as we help couples plan their families. Unfortunately, sometimes we overlook this fact, and we should not. For example, when I was in charge of USAID Global Health, which included programs on family planning, we were careful to have a variety of methods available to be sensitive to cultural and religious environments.

Since joining World Vision in 2011, I have witnessed consistent integration of HTSP into World Vision's maternal, neonatal, and child health (MNCH) programming, particularly in our 7–11 Global Health and Nutrition Strategy instituted in 2007, because we have outlined seven and eleven high impact interventions for mothers and children under two years respectively. The 7–11 Nutrition Strategy is being implemented in thirty-six countries.

We also implemented the USAID-funded Integrated Birth Spacing Project between 2007 and 2012 in India, Senegal, Burundi, and Haiti, where HTSP/family planning information and services were integrated

---

1. UNICEF, *Committing to Child Survival: A Promise Renewed—Progress Report 2014* (New York: UNICEF, 2013).

into ongoing MNCH programs. The results in all four countries showed an increase in family planning use by women of reproductive age who visited local government-run health facilities.

In 2013, World Vision launched the MOMENT[2] Project, a family planning and advocacy enterprise. The project aims to improve MNCH by increasing World Vision's engagement and political advocacy for global health (with a focus on MNCH and HTSP) and encourages the United States and Canadian governments to maintain robust global health funding commitments. In addition to this global advocacy work, World Vision uses its community-led advocacy initiative — Citizen Voice and Action — in India and Kenya to promote and increase use of available MNCH and HTSP/family planning services to improve child survival and women's health, prevent unintended pregnancies, and reduce child and maternal morbidity and mortality.

The country-led advocacy work combines providing information and services with the aim of creating a movement of communities that understand the benefits of practicing HTSP, how to achieve HTSP through use of voluntary family planning services, and where to seek family planning services and commodities. These communities also have the desire to continue practicing HTSP to affect better survival outcomes for children and mothers for generations to come. We have work to do — one-quarter and one-fifth of married women in Kenya and India respectively have unmet need[3] for family planning.

A key component of MOMENT is supporting faith leaders to understand why HTSP/FP is important so that they, in turn, can help influence their faith communities. World Vision's approach to working with faith leaders is through its Corridors of Hope Strategy, which directly addresses faith leaders' misconceptions around sensitive issues such as family planning and HIV/AIDS. Channels of Hope has successfully transformed faith communities and individuals to help ensure that the most vulnerable can experience fullness of life.

---

2. MOMENT—mobilizing for maternal and neonatal health through birth spacing and advocacy.

3. Unmet need for family planning is defined as the percentage of women who do not want to become pregnant but are not using contraception. See www.unpopulation.org.

Consider Abasi, a pastor in Kenya. When we first met him, he was known for taking a strong stand that birth was in God's hands and no man should interfere. Therefore, he encouraged the women in his village to avoid family planning and birth spacing. Furthermore, he felt that the proper course of action for a difficult labor or sick child was prayer, and prayer alone—not realizing that perhaps the answer God was granting to his prayer was the medical team available to help these women and children. Then, in 2014 he was invited to one of our seminars, and he says his "eyes were opened." He realized that even he, a pastor with a large family, was struggling to feed his children. So, together with other pastors, he worked to develop a scriptural validation message covering topics such as "Birth Spacing and God's Will" and "Does Family Planning Encourage Promiscuity?" He provided his congregation with Scripture to support and encourage parents to plan their pregnancies responsibly so that they could take care of themselves and their children to God's glory. This man, who was once staunchly opposed to HTSP, is now one of its best ambassadors.

We recognize the important positive connections among voluntary family planning and birth spacing, good maternity care, and child health and nutrition. To achieve these synergies, it is our duty as a faith community to provide information and services on HTSP to women, couples, and communities to contribute to better health outcomes for women and children worldwide.

Dr. Kent R. Hill is the senior vice president of international programs group for World Vision US and the former assistant administrator of the Bureau for Global Health for USAID. He lives in Manassas, Virginia.

Chapter 12

Personal and Professional Reasons to Be Thankful for Child Spacing

◄○► *Ray Martin*

I have an intimately personal reason for being a strong advocate for child spacing and family planning for the survival and health of women and children. I come from a Pennsylvania Mennonite farm family with two God-fearing parents and seven children. I am in the middle. I long ago noted that there were only two years' spacing between my three older siblings, but there were four years between my next older sibling and me.

Why? Well, when my mother was one hundred years old and I was seventy, she apparently thought I was mature enough to hear the explanation. She revealed that after three closely spaced babies, she was simply tired and felt her body was not ready for another pregnancy. She wanted to wait awhile to regain her strength. Back in the 1930s, the kind of contraceptive options now available did not exist. My parents did not even understand well the workings of the menstrual cycle. So my father, out of respect to my mother and with concern for her health, agreed not to have sexual intercourse for an extended period.

Eventually, they were ready again, and I am the healthy result, thanks to their care. I find my parents' sacrifice deeply touching, but my wish for any loving marriage today would be for access to information and methods to help avoid the sacrifice and stress they likely suffered.

In my lifetime career living in several African countries and Pakistan, serving with Mennonite Voluntary Service, USAID, the World Bank, and now as executive director of Christian Connections for International Health (CCIH), a large network of Christians promoting global health and wholeness from a Christian perspective, I have similarly encountered mothers and fathers who wanted to have healthy families and asked for help in spacing their pregnancies.

I asked myself, "What would Jesus do?" I believe that today he would support such measures that save the lives and improve the health of mothers and babies and enhance life and overall family well-being.

At CCIH, we are convinced that good, evidence-based public health is wholly consistent with faithfulness to God's Word. We define family planning as "enabling couples to determine the number and timing of pregnancies, including the voluntary use of methods for preventing pregnancy, not including abortion, harmonious with their values and religious beliefs." We know that 222 million women who say they want to avoid or delay a pregnancy lack access to family planning methods (natural and hormonal methods) to safely space the births of their children.

We work with our members in actively advocating for including family planning in maternal and child health programs and HIV/AIDS programs. We know that preventing unintended pregnancies among women living with HIV would significantly decrease the number of HIV-infected children. We help our members in Africa and around the world improve their service delivery programs and engage with local church leaders to educate their congregations on protecting their health. We urge the United States government to generously fund such programs in developing countries.

We respect the right of each couple or religious community to choose the methods for child spacing that are appropriate for them. We are absolute that family planning and abortion are two completely separate issues. We know that by avoiding unintended, poorly timed, and high-risk pregnancies, family planning reduces abortions. Some 210 million women across the globe become pregnant each year. Eighty million of those are unintended pregnancies. Around the world, 44 million women have induced abortions, and 47,000 women die each year as a result of unsafe abortions. Family planning reduces abortions.

In addition to supporting a range of contraceptives as chosen voluntarily by individuals or by the programs of our members, CCIH also advocates for vigorous programs to promote natural family planning methods, which have been shown to be effective when couples are motivated and properly educated in their use.

CCIH members working in the poorest regions of the world offer family planning services to help couples plan and space pregnancies to maximize the health of mothers, babies, and families. Typically these services are integrated with other health services to provide holistic health care as well as for efficiency in service delivery. We observe that these programs reduce both maternal and child mortality and reduce abortions. Data show that in areas where family planning methods are used by the greatest number of women, abortion rates are lower than in those areas where only a small proportion of women have access to family planning methods.

Protecting the health of mothers and their children and preventing abortions through avoiding unintended pregnancies should be obvious goals for Christians. Let's use our knowledge and resources, and the influence we have among faith communities across the globe, to help mothers and children have life—and have it abundantly.

Ray Martin is executive director emeritus of Christian Connections for International Health, a global network of Christian organizations and individuals promoting global health and wholeness from a Christian perspective. He has fifty years' experience in international health and development as a Mennonite volunteer in Africa, as chief of several USAID Health offices, and with the World Bank.

Chapter 13

Why Christians Should Care About Maternal Health

◄○► *Shepherd and Anita Smith*

As a Christian couple we are a bit unusual in that we became involved in the HIV/AIDS issue in the 1980s and, since that time, have dedicated our lives to helping those affected by this particular disease.

Throughout more than twenty-seven years of that caring process, we discovered many other issues that require our attention. While we both were familiar with the many references in Scripture that call us not to pass by those who are in need, but to stop and help them, neither of us ever thought we would end up where we are today: helping those who suffer from HIV/AIDS and also being proponents of maternal and child health. But that is what God was calling us to do, and that is what we have done.

In Africa in 1995, we traveled to South Africa and Malawi for the first time to better understand the HIV/AIDS crisis there. At the time, South Africa under apartheid had largely curtailed their epidemic, compared with nearby countries, by having strict restrictions on travel from neighboring nations and aggressive HIV testing of mine workers, prostitute populations, and prenatal clinics. However, with travel restrictions lifted as apartheid ended, South Africa was beginning to see a small rise in HIV infections among women presenting at prenatal clinics. Because South Africa was reluctant to acknowledge HIV in their society, people at that time were hidden and afraid.

At our specific request, we visited a home for HIV-positive women and an orphanage for children orphaned by HIV. The taxi driver dropped us off at the end of the road because he did not want to go anywhere near people with HIV, so we walked to both facilities. The experience was profound. The women were trying to make enough funds to support themselves through embroidery (which we purchased in abundance), and the orphanage was housing more than two times the number of children it was built to sustain. Walking out of that orphanage with dozens of toddlers raising their arms to us just wanting to be held was one of the most heart-wrenching things we've ever experienced.

From there we traveled to Malawi, where we were faced with a much more mature epidemic, in which HIV-infected people had already progressed to AIDS or died in large numbers.

Just a few years later, we traveled to Uganda, where we found an epidemic similar to that of Malawi. These were epidemics not driven by poverty, but—as in all areas of the world—instead fueled primarily through an increased number of sexual partners. At the time, data showed that, in a hospital in Kinshasa, infection rates among doctors, nurses, janitors, and patients of all economic backgrounds were roughly the same. In Malawi and Uganda we found college professors, medical professionals, government workers, and others at the high end of the economic ladder dying in numbers similar to, or larger than, the number of people dying in the working class community. Both countries were desperate for a solution to the scourge of HIV/AIDS.

Through a professional colleague we identified a rural mission hospital in Malawi, serving roughly 250,000 people, that would be an excellent model for clinical care and prevention. As we surveyed the needs of the 600 local villages in the catchment area the hospital served, it became apparent that HIV/AIDS was not the only problem facing these wonderful people. Maternal and child health became obvious and critical needs because of the high rate of both morbidity and mortality facing women and children. So in conjunction with the hospital leadership, we devised a comprehensive plan, implemented in 2000–2001, to encourage mothers to deliver their babies in the hospital (St. Gabriel's) and have them tested voluntarily for HIV after comprehensive counseling.

In addition, the fathers were able to take home nutritious meals along with their wives and children. This also provided the opportunity to offer voluntary testing to the fathers in a critical initiative we called family-centered care. Within a year, the 600 villages had established twenty

AIDS Health Councils, where critical information was disseminated on AIDS and other health issues. In just a few short years, deliveries at St. Gabriel's Hospital rose from 1,500 a year to more than 4,500. And unlike with most HIV programs, men became integral to its effectiveness. When the President's Emergency Plan for AIDS Relief was enacted in 2003, we were able to expand on the family-centered care clinics we had already established with local partners in Zambia, Uganda, and South Africa.

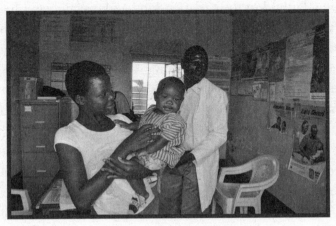

It was clear to us that the importance of child spacing is central to improving child and maternal health, and managing the reproductive cycle is fundamental to that happening. In addition, we found that non-abortive contraception, whether natural or artificial, is critical to that discussion. In many cases we brought in trained professionals to augment our efforts — professionals who would be sensitive to the cultural and religious needs of our clients.

After our nearly twenty years of working in sub-Saharan Africa with a number of care models, it is absolutely clear to us that the family-centered approach is essential. Programs focusing only on women and children that leave out the fathers will not have a long-term impact. This is true for HIV/AIDS, family planning, nutrition, clean water, and myriad other issues. Leaving out the male in the household most often defies the cultural context, but also sets up division within the household. As Christians, we believe it is critical to promote the strength of the family unit, which ensures better health and long-term outcomes, not just for the children, but for every member of the family.

In addition, we also appreciate and respect the sensitivities of various faith traditions. Interestingly, most faith traditions also focus on the importance of the family unit for health and well-being. We have seen the results of this approach: fewer maternal and child deaths; lower rates of HIV infections, due largely to young people delaying sexual debut and to adults being faithful in their relationships; and overall better health outcomes. It has been our honor to serve these amazing brothers and sisters around the globe. It should be no surprise to those of us who love Christ to see that recognition of the family unit is core to preserving good health for all people.

We hope that this model will be replicated more broadly and that others in God's kingdom will become aware that improving child and maternal health will reap great rewards when done within the framework of Scripture. We reflect on those orphans in South Africa who were craving love and attention, the thousands of precious people we have met in multiple countries (most of whom love the Lord), the compelling data related to maternal and child health, and Christ's example and admonitions for emulating his example—and rather than asking, "Why should Christians care about maternal health?" the question should be, "How can Christians not care?"

Shepherd Smith is the president of the Institute for Youth Development. His wife, Anita, is a writer and researcher and a co-chair of the Presidential Advisory Council on HIV and AIDS.

Chapter 14

Contraception Uncoupled

◄○► *Joe McIlhaney*

As an ob-gyn, my growing awareness of "life" in the womb accelerated when three other physicians and I founded one of the first truly successful, non-university in vitro fertilization (IVF) programs in the United States, in Austin, Texas, in 1984.

I made many other observations during those heady days of research and innovation. One was ultimately to change the course of my life and work. I began realizing that for many of our patients who were so infertile that their only chance for pregnancy was IVF—that they were in that condition because of damage to their fallopian tubes from the sexually transmitted infection (STI) chlamydia.

In 1992, I founded the Medical Institute for Sexual Health, and I left my medical practice in 1995 in order to run the organization. Much more important, I wanted to use the rest of my professional career to warn young people of the risks to their futures they were taking by being involved with multiple sexual partners. In our research and education and behavior guidance we were and are highly committed to following sexual behavior science wherever it leads. We want to follow that lead so we can deliver the very best message for young people.

Clearly, the very healthiest and safest sexual behavior, which we encouraged and still encourage, is to avoid sexual involvement unless married. As a fallback, we encourage limiting the number of lifetime sexual partners to as few as possible. We have never opposed the use of condoms or contraceptives, but we want to educate young people to know that these techniques, at the individual level, do not totally protect against either pregnancy or STIs. We felt—and still do feel—that young people deserve full sexual health information, and through the years we have worked to provide it.

It is important for an individual to be aware of this information so they can make their own personal best decision about their sexual behavior. Though none of these techniques prevents the risk of STI or of pregnancy, they certainly reduce the risk of these occurrences. We will discuss the fact that the broad use of these techniques can reduce the risk of both disease, including HIV, and of pregnancy in a community or country. But first I would like to very briefly discuss some of the controversy surrounding the use of contraceptives.

First, oral contraceptives are essentially safe. Any drug that is given to millions of people will occasionally result in a few people having unfortunate reactions. However, the number of women who have been saved from problems of pregnancy far outweigh any unfortunate results in the lives of the few women who have been affected in an unhealthy way by "the pill."

The intrauterine device (IUD) may possibly cause the loss of a fertilized egg (an embryo). I personally consider an embryo a human being. However, the science about whether IUDs do indeed cause the loss of embryos is far from clear. Many very pro-life physicians feel that it is legitimate and ethical to insert IUDs; many do not.

When one looks at the low pregnancy rates found in women who use IUDs and that IUDs can remain in the woman's uterus for years without any special care, one can see the advantage of IUD use. It is clear that the primary way the IUD works is to make the environment in the uterus hostile to both egg and sperm and to kill those cells before fertilization can occur.

Depo-Provera is injectable progesterone designed to prevent pregnancy. Yet it has a pregnancy rate that is a little higher than one would expect. This is almost for sure, because a woman must get the injection every three months, or she is prone to become pregnant. Women can have other problems with the use of Depo-Provera, such as acne, weight gain, not having periods for months after stopping the use of the drug, and the inconvenience of seeing a health care provider every three months. For those women who can access Depo-Provera, who have the self-discipline to get injections on time, and who do not have physical problems with the drug, it is a quite effective contraceptive.

International efforts to increase contraceptive use worldwide have often been, at times, simultaneously coupled with abortion. That being said, the Helms Amendment of 1973 prohibits the use of US foreign assistance to pay for the performance of abortion as a method of family planning or to motivate or coerce any person to practice abortion. Though the United States does not couple contraception and abortion, often the two are conflated. In separating the two issues, it is important to know that contraceptive technology can be lifesaving in multiple ways when broadly used.

The United Nations has recently set new international goals for health and development, titled "Sustainable Development Goals." The problem of preventable maternal mortality is:

> Although maternal deaths worldwide have decreased by 45% since 1990, 800 women still die each day from largely preventable causes before, during, and after the time of birth. These deaths are not equally distributed. Ninety-nine percent of preventable maternal deaths occur in low and middle income countries. Within countries, risk of death is disproportionately high among the most vulnerable segments of the society.[1]

These are the individuals, humans, people made in the image of God, who are most likely to suffer the problems of childbirth.

And the issues don't stop with death. Many of the young women in developing countries who become pregnant still have very young bodies, too small for childbirth. The grinding of the baby's head against the bones of a small pelvis with the bladder (and even the rectum) caught between can cause a hole to be worn between the vagina and the bladder or between the vagina and the rectum. This results in a vesicovaginal or rectovaginal fistula.

The problem from this, then, is lifelong drainage of either urine or stool or both. This makes the young woman miserable. She may become an outcast. She may smell. She may not ever be able to marry. And in sub-Saharan Africa alone, there are so many women living with this problem that there is no way, even with all the missionary doctors or visiting surgeons from medical schools, that all of these fistulae can be repaired.

---

1. http://who.int/reproductivehealth/topics/maternal_prenatal/Strategies_EPMM_COMMENTS.pdf.

Contraception can help. Though it fails a lot more than most realize, for both disease and pregnancy, if it is used broadly in a community or a country, it *will* help to reduce incidence of both. Broad implementation of contraceptive programs can help the individual and impact the society. These programs should be able to help reduce poverty, hunger, disease including HIV, and death.

Indeed, contraception can help the individual and the family in so many ways. It can give them the opportunity to rise out of poverty. It can help them reduce the likelihood that they will have a child die by reducing the number of children they are responsible for feeding. It can help a young woman delay childbearing until her body is mature enough to deliver a baby, thus eliminating damage that might occur because of childbirth.

The opportunity to help some of the most downtrodden people in the world is therefore enormous. If we can uncouple contraception from abortion in our assumptions and perceptions, much good can result. Indeed, it would be wise even to follow the lead of in-country programs. If we could see these countries and communities with a new attitude of humility—seeing these communities, even in the slums, as composed of individuals of great worth, made in the image of God, who have their own vital faith and integrity—then cooperation can really take off.

If we can uncouple contraception from abortion in our assumptions and perceptions, much good can result.

With cooperation can come teaching and understanding and acceptance. Opportunity is available. Let's grasp it!

Joe McIlhaney, MD, is the founder and president of the Medical Institute for Sexual Health. He lives in central Texas with his wife of fifty-three years. They have three daughters and ten grandchildren.

Chapter 15

From Mother to Mother

◄○► *Kimberly Williams-Paisley*

After the Haitian earthquake in January 2010, I watched TV images of orphaned children and distraught adults crying, terrified, and mutilated. It was horrifying, but at the same time, remote. My heart ached for these people, but aside from sending money to a relief organization, I'm embarrassed to admit, I didn't think a lot more about how I might be able to help them.

Instead, I thought about my own life. My aging parents. My son, Huck, starting at a new preschool. My schedule, married as much as possible to my husband's busy schedule as a music artist on the road. Not to mention my commitments to helping some of my fellow Tennesseans who were struggling with their own challenges, including hunger and children's health. It was too painful to agonize over people's troubles in a foreign country. I turned off the television. I shut it out. *This has nothing to do with me,* I thought.

Across town, one of my best friends, Tracie Hamilton, couldn't turn away from the news the way I could. Haiti became a kind of obsession to her. She kept looking for a way to help. A couple of years later, she met Dr. David and Laurie Vanderpool, who were taking regular groups to Thomazeau, just outside of Port-au-Prince, with their relief organization, LiveBeyond.

Tracie signed up for a trip. When she came back a week later, I could tell she had changed. She raved about the loving people, the colorful sunsets, and even the lukewarm Haitian coffee. I sensed in her a new purpose. She asked if I wanted to go on the next trip with her. But my husband, Brad, was recording an album, my son Jasper was having night terrors, and I had planned a couple of trips to New York to see my parents. *This has nothing to do with me,* I kept thinking.

When Tracie came back a few months later from a second trip, even more ecstatic, she gave me updates on all of her new friends. So I let my in-laws take care of the boys for a night, and I agreed to come to her house to meet the Vanderpools and hear them speak about their work in Haiti. Instantly, I was struck by their spirit. Their family loves and lives for God. Their faith motivates every step they take, every word they speak, every hug they give, openly and freely.

Dr. Vanderpool explained the plight of the Haitians, who are living in what many consider to be the poorest country in the world. I saw the same sense of purpose in David and Laurie that I'd recently seen in Tracie. It was contagious. He showed us pictures of little children, mothers, babies, even emaciated animals. He told us about the lack of access to clean water and how that affects everything from health to education, because children are sent miles away to fetch it. He told us about staggering infant and maternal mortality rates.

"The Haitians desperately need our help," he said. And then he reminded us that their country is just an hour and a half away from our border. *We are talking about our neighbors.*

At first I thought, *Well, yes! Okay! I will send them money.*

But David was asking for more than financial support. To my surprise, he went on to plead for volunteers willing to make the trip. "We need your time," he said. "We need your energy. We need your hands-on volunteerism."

This was scary. Go to Haiti? It seemed like a total detour. *This has nothing to do with me!* But there was something about that infectious light I saw in Tracie, Laurie, David, and everyone else who spoke that night — a God-given joy that comes from helping others. Helping our neighbors. It finally hit me: *Make Haiti have something to do with you.*

I got my mosquito net and my shots. I would be allowed one carry-on for the week. My checked luggage allowance would be used for supplies. We would be doing medical clinics and dispersing food, prayer, and love. I heard about the cold, drippy shower that backs up in the drain in the guesthouse where we'd be staying. I was told to bring lots of baby wipes, hand sanitizer, sunscreen, Deet. "Zip up your sleeping bag at night," they said, because sometimes there were rats. *Good Lord, what was I getting into?* I was an Episcopalian from New York who had never had to pray out loud in front of a group of people and had *never* been on a missions trip.

But at 4:30 a.m. one cool June morning in 2012, I kissed my sleeping boys on the forehead. *This will be good for them*, I told myself. *This will be good for me.* I took my Bible and my overstuffed carry-on and shut the door to my cozy home and headed for Haiti.

Hot, humid, and 100-degree air, smelling a little of oil, wafted through the plane as the doors opened up to the tarmac in Haiti. I was surprised to see a small band playing as we marched into the noisy, crowded terminal to claim our worn LiveBeyond bags filled with supplies we would need for the week. Our group of about twenty-five volunteers got into a caravan of trucks and headed down the rocky dirt road toward Thomazeau.

One day in one of the clinics, I found myself treating scabies, a parasite that spreads easily, causes sores on the skin, and can lead to disease if left untreated. Our tiny, windowless room was full of people—especially children—who needed help. Almost everyone had scabies, but we also saw ringworm, burns, deep wounds, infections, and scarred feet that have never worn shoes. Almost all of these people were hungry, many starving. The phrase I heard most often was "*mwen grengu*": I'm hungry.

> **What struck me more than anything was the love I saw between mothers and their children. It moved me because I recognized it.**

But what struck me more than anything was the love I saw between mothers and their children. It moved me because I recognized it. *I* feel that love for *my* children. *I* feel that love for *my* parents. It's a simple idea, but it was life-changing to see it in this group of people who I thought had nothing to do with me and my life. It hit me hard. *These people matter.*

I used my own skills as a mom as I applied ringworm shampoo, taking care to keep it out of a child's eyes. I gave out Band-Aids and lollipops to help calm fears. These people had none of the choices that my children had. Most of them had seen more tragedy in their short lives than I may ever see. They spent many of their days sick. They'd never had access to clean drinking water, food had never been abundant, and they'd never had adequate shelter or health care.

I wasn't able to help everyone. We had to turn people away at the end of each day. Nor did I come close to solving the seemingly insurmountable challenges Haiti faces. But because I chose to go there, maybe twenty-five more people were treated at the clinic each day. I was able to show simple kindness to this small group, if only for a few minutes. Laurie and David reminded us often to love the ones in front of us. To give them hope for a better life after this one. The surprise was how much these Haitians (whom I was supposed to be helping) were blessing *me*. Inspiring *me*. Helping *me* to grow in a new sense of purpose. I am profoundly grateful to them.

Jericho is a child I will not soon forget, although I probably spent less time with him than anyone else. He was born with encephalitis and lived with it his whole life. When I saw him, he was about ten or eleven, lying on a straw mat on the ground in his hut next to his mother, covered by a thin white sheet. He was five days away from death. I could not imagine him living a minute longer than he did when I saw him. My heart breaks when I think of what those days must have been like for him. His head was much larger than it should have been. He was conscious. His eyes were open, darting around the room, and his bony hands trembled. His mother lifted off the sheet, and I gasped when I saw his ribs protruding above his concave belly. I had never seen in person a body like his of skin and bones.

What makes me saddest is that if Jericho had had the care we have available in the United States, his condition could have been taken care of when he was a baby. He could have had a normal life. But there is no health care system set up yet in Thomazeau, Haiti.

Globally, more than 6.6 million children under the age of five died during 2013. These children died from pneumonia, diarrhea, or malaria. More than 40 percent of these children were newborns. With vaccines, basic antibiotics, oral rehydration therapies, bed nets, and primary care, these children would have had a chance at life. These are simple, cheap solutions to preventable, treatable issues.

I came home from Haiti changed. My husband and I got very involved with a water project, partnering with LiveBeyond, aimed at providing access to clean water for the 200,000 people of Thomazeau. I have been back to the country twice since my first trip, and I plan to go again soon. I miss being there. I miss being able to connect with these beautiful people. I miss seeing the moon at night and knowing it is the same moon over my two boys asleep in their beds back in Tennessee. I even miss the lukewarm Haitian coffee.

I look forward to coming home next time with fresh stories, to share with my children, of these people who live in a very different place. To plant the seed in my boys' hearts. To teach them to care about the poor and the needy, no matter where they are in the world.

I am enormously inspired by people like Tracie and the Vanderpools who walk with God in all of the decisions they make, and I see the way that blesses them.

Jesus called on us over and over to help the poor. Visit widows and orphans in their trouble: James 1:27. Whoever is generous to the poor lends to the Lord: Proverbs 19:17.

So what does this have to do with *you*?

Will you make the people of Haiti matter to you? Will you grab a mosquito net and join me? Can you imagine how many more people will have hope because you loved them, through prayer or medicine or Band-Aids or advocacy? How many people like Jericho and his mother will have better lives because you made an effort?

Decide with me to care about these mothers and children. Decide with me to do something.

First, you can always give. Give your money, your time, and yourself. Go to LiveBeyond.org to learn more about how you can help families in Thomazeau, Haiti, with health care or clean water.

Second, share this message with your family, friends, and community. Raising awareness through your social networks or events at school or church is a powerful way to educate and activate Americans about global health issues.

Finally, share your voice. Our legislators and policymakers need to hear from you. They need to hear that their constituents care about maternal and child health issues around the world. Consider calling or writing your representative today.

If we lift our voices together on behalf of the world's poorest, we can save the lives of millions. The irony is that the richest blessing will most likely be your own.

Kimberly Williams-Paisley is a writer and an actor, known especially for her roles in Father of the Bride, According to Jim, *and* Nashville. *She is working on a book about her family's struggle with her mother's dementia. She and her husband, Brad Paisley, are actively involved with development projects in Haiti. She has been an advocate for children's health locally and abroad for over ten years. She lives in Nashville, Tennessee.*

Part 2

Strong Mothers

◄○►

*The Key to Healthy Families,
Communities, and Nations*

Beryl Anyango's Story
Kenya

It was due to tireless efforts by my lady pastor that I can now smile at my fourteen-month-old baby boy.

My troubles began in 2009 when I got married to a young man of my dreams whom I really loved. But the relationship was not to last, since I immediately became pregnant. I started bleeding and was in pain, but did not know what to do or from whom to seek help. As young as we were, we did nothing to stop the bleeding and pain. At five months I miscarried the baby.

Three months later I again conceived, and the problem reoccurred. But thanks to the church at which I was a member, the pastor spotted me, how pale I looked, and sent me to the hospital. There I received treatment and was put on observation. I had to report every two weeks for treatment. I did not want to lose my second child, so I requested to be released to go to the national capital in Nairobi, where I could have access to the big referral hospital.

I followed the doctor's advice, and when the time for delivery came, I ended up in Kenyatta National Hospital in Nairobi to undergo a C-section. I delivered a baby girl, and I was overjoyed. Before I was discharged, I was encouraged by the health workers at Kenyatta hospital to go to the family planning clinic to prevent another pregnancy so that I could take care of my baby and myself. I did so and chose the pill.

After my baby was about three months old, I went back to my village. But my joy did not last as my baby started being sick. After several visits to the local hospital and testing, my baby was diagnosed with sickle-cell disease.

It was at this point that my relationship with my husband and his family started going downhill. I was accused of not being able to bear a healthy child, and my husband left me for another woman when my baby girl died at eight months. For a whole year I did not see my husband, but during this period the church stood by me and supported and encouraged me.

My husband came back after a year, I conceived, and he left again. Of course I had stopped taking the pill after my baby girl died. This time I carried the pregnancy to term without any problems and delivered a healthy baby boy whom I named Samuel. During my pregnancy I attended all my clinics as advised and practiced exclusive breastfeeding. My baby grew up healthy to my amazement and that of many. Though Samuel's father, my husband, never came back, I am taking good care of myself and Samuel. I sell used clothing at the Siaya town center to take care of my son and myself.

This year I learned through my pastor more about maternal, newborn, and child health (MNCH) and then about healthy timing and spacing of pregnancies (HTSP) and family planning (FP). My pastor was trained in World Vision's Channels of Hope methodology, which addresses faith leaders' misconceptions about sensitive issues such as family planning, and now she and the church leaders are helping me, other women in our community, and the congregants to make right choices.

I am now using a family planning method—Depo-Provera injection—to help me prevent a pregnancy, because I want Samuel to grow up healthy and strong. I often recall my experience with the two pregnancies. I do not want to repeat the mistakes I made, and now I am always ready to tell other women about maternal and child health, healthy spacing and timing of pregnancies, and family planning messages that are being shared in the community to help protect and help women and children survive and thrive.

This is a message I want my sisters in the United States to know about. Because my pastor learned about the benefits of MNCH and HTSP/FP services, my baby and I are alive and well.

Chapter 16

Helping Women Isn't Just a "Nice" Thing to Do

<o> *Hillary Clinton*

Speech given at the Women in the World Summit in New York City, April 2013. Opening remarks omitted.

I have always believed that women are not victims, we are agents of change, we are drivers of progress, we are makers of peace—all we need is a fighting chance.

And that firm faith in the untapped potential of women at home and around the world has been at the heart of my work my entire life, from college and law school, from Arkansas to the White House to the Senate. And when I became Secretary of State, I was determined to weave this perspective even deeper into the fabric of American foreign policy.

But I knew to do that, I couldn't just preach to the usual choir. We had to reach out, not only to men, in solidarity and recruitment, but to religious communities, to every partner we could find. We had to make the case to the whole world that creating opportunities for women and girls advances security and prosperity for everyone. So we relied on the empirical research that shows that when women participate in the economy, everyone benefits. When women participate in peace-making and peace-keeping, we are all safer and more secure. And when women participate in politics of their nations, they can make a difference.

But as strong a case as we've made, too many otherwise thoughtful people continue to see the fortunes of women and girls as somehow separate from society at large. They nod, they smile, and then they relegate these issues once again to the sidelines. I have seen it over and over again; I have been kidded about it; I have been ribbed; I have been challenged in boardrooms and official offices across the world.

But fighting to give women and girls a fighting chance isn't a nice thing to do. It isn't some luxury that we get to when we have time on our hands to spend. This is a core imperative for every human being in every society. If we do not continue the campaign for women's rights and opportunities, the world we want to live in, the country we all love and cherish, will not be what it should be.

It is no coincidence that so many of the countries that threaten regional and global peace are the very places where women and girls are deprived of dignity and opportunity. Think of the young women from northern Mali to Afghanistan whose schools have been destroyed. Or of the girls across Africa, the Middle East, and South Asia who have been condemned to child marriage. Or of the refugees of the conflicts from eastern Congo to Syria who endure rape and deprivation as a weapon of war.

It is no coincidence that so many of the countries where the rule of law and democracy are struggling to take root are the same places where women and girls cannot participate as full and equal citizens. Like in Egypt, where women stood on the front lines of the revolution, but are now being denied their seats at the table and face a rising tide of sexual violence.

I have always believed that women are not victims. We are agents of change, we are drivers of progress, we are makers of peace — all we need is a fighting chance.

It is no coincidence that so many of the countries making the leap from poverty to prosperity are places now grappling with how to empower women. I think it is one of the unanswered questions of the rest of this century to whether countries, like China and India, can sustain their growth and emerge as true global economic powers. Much of that depends on what happens to women and girls.

None of these are coincidences. Instead, they demonstrate—and your presence here confirms—that we are meeting at a remarkable moment of confluence.

Because in countries and communities across the globe where for generations violence against women has gone unchecked, opportunity and dignity virtually unknown, there is a powerful new current of grass-roots activism stirring, galvanized by events too outrageous to ignore and enabled by new technologies that give women and girls voices like never before. That's why we need to seize this moment. But we need to be thoughtful and smart and savvy about what this moment really offers to us.

Now many of us have been working and advocating and fighting for women and girls for more decades than we care to remember. And I think we can be and should be proud of all that we've achieved. Conferences like this one have been part of that progress. But let's recognize much of our advocacy is still rooted in a twentieth century, top-down frame. The world is changing beneath our feet, and it is past time to embrace a twenty-first-century approach to advancing the rights and opportunities of women and girls at home and across the globe.

Think about it. You know, technology, from satellite television to cell phones from Twitter to Tumblr, is helping bring abuses out of the shadows and into the center of global consciousness. Think of that woman in a blue bra beaten in Tahrir Square; think about that six-year-old girl in Afghanistan about to be sold into marriage to settle a family debt.

Just as importantly, technological changes are helping inspire, organize, and empower grassroots action. I have seen this, and that is where progress is coming from, and that's where our support is needed. We have a tremendous stake in the outcome of these metrics.

Today, more than ever, we see clearly that the fate of women and girls around the world is tied up with the greatest security and economic challenges of our time.

Consider Pakistan, a proud country with a rich history that recently marked a milestone in its democratic development when a civilian government completed its full term for the very first time. It is no secret that Pakistan is plagued by many ills: violent extremism, sectarian conflict, poverty, energy shortages, corruption, weak democratic institutions. It is a combustible mix. And more than 30,000 Pakistanis have been killed by terrorists in the last decade.

The repression of women in Pakistan exacerbates all of these problems.

More than 5 million children do not attend school—and two-thirds of them are girls. The Taliban insurgency has made the situation even worse.

As Malala has said and reminded us: "We live in the twenty-first century. How can we be deprived from education?" She went on to say, "I have the right to play. I have the right to sing. I have the right to talk. I have the right to go to market. I have the right to speak up."

How many of us here today would have that kind of courage? The Taliban recognized this young girl, fourteen years at the time, as a serious threat. You know what? They were right—she was a threat. Extremism thrives amid ignorance and anger, intimidation and cowardice. As Malala said, "If this new generation is not given pens, they will be given guns."

But the Taliban miscalculated. They thought if they silenced Malala—and thank God they didn't—that not only she, but her cause would die. Instead, they inspired millions of Pakistanis to finally say, "Enough is enough." You heard it directly from those two brave young Pakistani women yesterday. And they are not alone. People marched in the streets and signed petitions demanding that every Pakistani child—girls as well as boys—have the opportunity to attend school. And that in itself was a rebuke to the extremists and their ideology.

I'm well aware that improving life for Pakistan's women is not a panacea. But it's impossible to imagine making real progress on the country's other problems—especially violent extremism—without tapping the talents and addressing the needs of Pakistan's women, including reducing corruption, ending the culture of impunity, expanding access to education, to credit, to all the tools that give a woman or a man make the most of their life's dreams. None of this will be easy or quick. But the grassroots response to Malala's shooting gives us hope for the future.

Again and again we have seen women drive peace and progress. In Northern Ireland, Catholic and Protestant women like Inez McCormack came together to demand an end to the Troubles and helped usher in the Good Friday Accords. In Liberia, women marched and protested until the country's warlords agreed to end their civil war; they prayed the devil back to hell; and they twice elected Ellen Johnson Sirleaf as the first woman president in Africa. An organization called Sisters Against Violent Extremism now connects women in more than a dozen countries who have risked their lives to tell terrorists that they are not welcome in their communities.

So the next time you hear someone say that the fate of women and girls is not a core national security issue, it's not one of those hard issues that really smart people deal with, remind them: The extremists understand the stakes of this struggle. They know that when women are liberated, so are entire societies. We must understand this too. And not only understand it, but act on it.

And the struggles do not end. Struggles do not end when countries attempt the transition to democracy. We've seen that very clearly the last few years.

Many millions, including many of us, were inspired and encouraged by the way women and men worked together during the revolutions in places like Egypt, Tunisia, and Libya. But we know that all over the world, when the dust settles, too often women's gains

> **Extremists know that when women are liberated, so are entire societies. We must understand this too. And not only understand it, but act on it.**

are lost to better organized, more powerful forces of oppression.

We see women largely shut out of decision-making. We see women activists believe they are being targeted by organized campaigns of violence and intimidation.

But still, many brave activists, women and men alike, continue to advocate for equality and dignity for all Egyptians, Tunisians, and Libyans. They know the only way to realize the promise of the Arab Spring is with and through the full participation of half the population.

Now, what is true in politics is also true in economics.

In the years ahead, a number of rapidly developing nations are poised to reshape the global economy, lift many millions out of poverty and into the middle class. This will be good for them and good for us—it will create vast new markets and trading partners.

But no country can achieve its full economic potential when women are left out or left behind ... a fact underscored day after day and, most recently to me, a tragedy in India.

Concerning the young twenty-three-year-old woman, brutally beaten and raped on a Delhi bus last December, she was from a poor farming family, but like so many women and men, she wanted to climb that economic ladder. She had aspirations for her life. She studied all day to become a physical therapist, then went to work at call centers in the evening. She slept two hours a night. President Mukherjee described her as a "symbol of all that New India strives to be."

But if her life embodied the aspirations of a rising nation, her death and her murder pointed to the many challenges still holding it back. The culture of rape is tied up with a broader set of problems: official corruption, illiteracy, inadequate education, laws and traditions, customs, and culture, that prevent women from being seen as equal human beings. And in addition, in many places — India and China being the leaders — in skewed gender balance with many more men than women, which contributes to human trafficking, child marriage, and other abuses that dehumanize women and corrode society.

So millions of Indians took to the streets in 2011; they protested corruption. In 2012 came the Delhi gang rape, and the two causes merged. Demands for stronger measures against rape were joined by calls for better policing and more responsive governance, for an India that could protect all its citizens and deliver the opportunities they deserve. Some have called that the "Indian Spring."

Because, as the protesters understood, India will rise or fall with its women. It's had a tradition of strong women leaders, but those women leaders, like women leaders around the world, like those who become presidents or prime ministers or foreign ministers or heads of corporations, cannot be seen as tokens that give everyone else in society the chance to say we've taken care of our women. So any country that wants to rise economically and improve productivity needs to open the doors.

Latin America and the Caribbean have steadily increased women's participation in the labor market since the 1990s; they now account for more than half of all workers. The World Bank estimates that extreme poverty in the region has decreased by 30 percent as a result.

Here in the United States, American women went from holding 37 percent of all jobs forty years ago to nearly 48 percent today. And the productivity gains attributable to this increase account for more than $3.5 trillion in GDP growth over those four decades. Similarly, fast-growing Asian economies could boost their per capita incomes by as much as 14 percent by 2020 if they brought more women into the workforce.

Laws and traditions that hold back women hold back entire societies. Creating more opportunities for women and girls will grow economies and spread prosperity. When I first began talking about this, using rape data from the World Bank and private sector analyses, there were doubters who couldn't quite put the pieces together. But that debate is over. Opening the doors to one's economy for women will make a difference.

Now, I want to conclude where I began, with the unfinished business we face here at home. The challenges and opportunities I've outlined today are not just for the people of the developing world. America must face this too, if we want to continue leading the world.

Traveling the globe these last four years reaffirmed and deepened my pride in our country and the ideals we represent. But it also challenged me to think about who we are and the values we are supposed to be living here at home in order to represent abroad. After all, our global leadership for peace and prosperity, for freedom and equality, is not a birthright. It must be earned by every generation.

And yes, we now have American women at high levels of business, academia, and government—you name it. But, as we've seen in recent months, we're still asking age-old questions about how to make women's way in male-dominated fields, how to balance the demands of work and family. *The Economist* magazine recently published what it called a "glass-ceiling index," ranking countries based on factors like opportunities for women in the workplace and equal pay. The United States was not even in the top ten. Worse, recent studies have found that, on average, women live shorter lives in America than in any other major industrialized country.

Think about it for a minute. We are the richest and most powerful country in the world. Yet many American women today are living shorter lives than their mothers, especially those with the least education. That is a historic reversal that rivals the decline in life expectancy for Russian men after the disintegration of the Soviet Union.

Now, there is no single explanation for why this is happening. Prescription drug overdoses have spiked: obesity, smoking, lack of health insurance, intractable poverty. But the fact is that for too many American women, opportunity and the dream of upward mobility—the American Dream—remains elusive.

That's not the way it's supposed to be. I think of the extraordinary sacrifices my mother made to survive her own difficult childhood, to give me not only life, but opportunity along with love and inspiration. And I'm very proud of my own daughter, and I look at all these young women I'm privileged to work with or know through Chelsea, and it's hard to imagine turning the clock back on them. But in places throughout America large and small, the clock is turning back.

So, we have work to do. Renewing America's vitality at home and strengthening our leadership abroad will take the energy and talents of all our people, women and men.

If America is going to lead, we need to learn from the women of the world who have blazed new paths and developed new solutions, on everything from economic development to education to environmental protection.

If America is going to lead, we need to catch up with so much of the rest of the world and finally ratify the UN Convention on the Elimination of All Discrimination Against Women.

If America is going to lead, we need to stand by the women of Afghanistan after our combat troops come home, we need to speak up for all the women working to realize the promise of the Arab Spring and do more to save the lives of the hundreds of thousands of mothers who die every year during childbirth from preventable causes and so much more.

But that's not all.

Because if America is going to lead, we expect ourselves to lead, we need to empower women here at home to participate fully in our economy and our society, we need to make equal pay a reality, we need to extend family and medical leave benefits to more workers and make them paid, and we need to encourage more women and girls to pursue careers in math and science.

We need to invest in our people so they can live up to their own God-given potential.

That's how America will lead in the world.

So let's learn from the wisdom of every mother and father all over the world who teaches their daughters that there is no limit on how big she can dream and how much she can achieve.

This truly is the unfinished business of the twenty-first century. And it is the work we are all called to do. I look forward to being your partner in all the days and years ahead. Let's keep fighting for opportunity and dignity; let's keep fighting for freedom and equality; let's keep fighting for full participation. And let's keep telling the world over and over again that, yes, women's rights are human rights, and human rights are women's rights once and for all.

———————————

Hillary Clinton is the former Secretary of State of the United States of America and a former First Lady of the United States. This transcript originally appeared on Women in the World, *April 2013. Used by permission.*

Chapter 17

Maternal Health and the Strategy for Empowering Women

◄○► *Bruce Wilkinson*

Mothers are the cornerstones on which families rest. Whether in New York or Nigeria, in the city or the countryside, in a developing or an industrialized nation, a healthy mother can expect to have healthier children.

The link between education and health is clear: Educated women are more likely to engage in healthy behavior and less likely to contract infections such as HIV. The effect is cumulative: When women are not able to complete their educations or work at jobs, when they are malnourished or ill, mortality rates increase for both mothers and their children. In the developing world especially, when mothers can't work, their children must become breadwinners—often at the expense of their health and always to the detriment of their educations.

While faith-based organizations (FBOs) may differ from non-FBOs in their approach to safe motherhood, everyone agrees that improving health for mothers means improving their economic and educational status. This, in turn, rests on their empowerment through family planning and birth spacing.

Studies have found that women who don't practice birth spacing suffer several health problems at much higher rates than those who do; these include obesity, hypertension, anemia, and low-limb edema. They are also less likely to survive childbirth. Preterm births are almost twice as frequent in families that didn't practice birth spacing, and children born more than three years since the last delivery are nearly 2.5 times more likely to live to age five than those born two years or less after a previous birth. The evidence is clear: birth spacing saves the lives of women and their children.

More than 220 million women worldwide do not have access to information about—let alone the services or tools necessary for—even the most rudimentary family planning. The most acute examples include South Sudan, where decades of war have destroyed the infrastructure necessary for education. As a result, 90 percent of women are illiterate. Birth rates are extremely high—and maternal mortality rates are the world's highest. One in seven South Sudanese women can expect to die from complications related to pregnancy or childbirth (compared with Sweden's lifetime maternal death risk of 1 in 13,600).

I have worked for thirty years to provide health care in the developing world, often with FBOs. My experience has convinced me that not only is it imperative for nongovernmental organizations to respond to this need, but also that FBOs, whose history of providing health care in remote or dangerous locations invests them with great trust and repute, are ideally positioned to lead that response. Indeed, while it might come as a surprise to many, FBOs often already fulfill that role.

In 1977 I was traveling between two work sites in Ghana when a couple flagged me down. The woman was in labor. She and her husband were trying to reach an FBO-run clinic nearly an hour away. In-facility births were even less common then in Africa than they are today, but this couple had been convinced by the care they received on a previous visit to return to the clinic for antenatal care. This included nutrition training, prenatal screening, and education about why it was best to give birth in a health care facility.

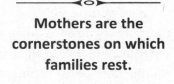

Mothers are the cornerstones on which families rest.

The FBO's advice also included recommendations about birth spacing, and it's a good thing for all of us that it did. The mother was in second-stage labor when I picked her up, and nature quickly took its course: she gave birth in my jeep. Because she had waited three years since her previous delivery, she was 125 percent more likely to survive childbirth. Combined with her other good antenatal practices, this drastically reduced her risk of obstetric emergency. When we reached the clinic, all that remained for the doctor to do was cut the umbilical cord. It's a happy story that could so easily have been a tragedy.

Given the importance of healthy mothers and families in breaking the cycle of poverty, the Catholic Medical Mission Board (CMMB) has chosen to begin our second century by narrowing our strategic focus so we can better improve the lives of women and children. We will do this by establishing Children and Mothers Partnerships (CHAMPS) with donors, other agencies, and local community groups and church health facilities in specific communities in need in Africa, Latin America, and the Caribbean.

Part of this CMMB strategy must be dedicated to the empowerment of women. This means economic empowerment, of course, but it also means helping women develop and master the knowledge and tools to manage their own health. Because of the incredible danger associated with too-frequent pregnancy, birth spacing is—and indeed, must be—at the forefront of our approach.

Bruce Wilkinson is the president and CEO of the Catholic Medical Mission Board. He is on the board of the Bill and Melinda Gates Foundation's Africa Malaria Initiative and is a member of the World Bank's Health, Nutrition, and Population Civil Society Consultative Group. He and his wife, Linda, have five children.

Chapter 18

Better Moms Make a Better World

<o> *Sherry Surratt*

The road swirled with dust, and the scorching heat made the air feel like a thick felt blanket. We were walking side by side—me and this mom of four from Mbita, Kenya. And while our destination of the day was the same, I knew our lives were very different. Monika and I were headed to her house for lunch after attending Sunday worship services, and we made a few stops. The first was to purchase a live chicken for butchering. The next was to carefully choose fresh greens and rice; Monika carefully inspected them for insects before making the purchases. The money exchange was quick and direct; Monika carefully negotiated each one.

We talked of life and motherhood as we walked on. Monika's children were healthy, and all attended school. She shared her dreams with me for extended schooling, which would allow them to go past the eighth grade. I could tell by her proud tone that this was a luxury.

In her one-room metal framed hut, I noted order, a sense of purposeful efficiency, from the makeshift desk that held one book and several pieces of charcoal for writing, to the tidy, cleanly swept kitchen space. While there were no beds, there was a designated sleeping area. Pallets neatly lined the wall, each with their own mosquito net. In the other homes I had visited, a sense of carelessness was evident, bereft of a sense of family or structure. Food remains were left haphazardly, with no evidence that members had meals together or slept in assigned sleeping areas. No proof of household chores existed, such as a thatch broom leaning again the wall or soap for cleaning dishes or hands. In Monika's house, each family member had evidence of belonging, and it was easy to interpret the household routine. Why was this home so different from the others I had visited? I began to ask questions.

The answers came when I learned the story of Lillian, a native Kenyan who served as the school's parent liaison. With no formal training, Lillian took it upon herself to make home visits, checking to see that the students had food to eat and a place to rest, that they had a designated spot in which to do their simple schoolwork, that water was boiled properly before drinking. Because Monica's children went to the school, she benefited from these visits.

When I accompanied Lillian on visits to other homes in the area, I observed her probing eyes and gentle touch as her hands searched the children for signs of malaria or worms. She sat with each mom, speaking in her native language, giving gentle advice and encouragement, sometimes leaving food or bars of homemade soap. She encouraged the moms to talk about the things they were learning with the other moms in the village and to encourage them to bring their children to the village school. Lillian's concern stretched beyond the boundaries of the children who attended—her attention focused on the moms.

As the CEO of MOPS International, I know that moms are a catalyst of health and well-being in the family. After studying the forty years of MOPS research, I now know what Lillian seemed to instinctively know: Moms become better moms when they receive basic training, help, and encouragement, and the impact stretches beyond the walls of the family hut.

The common thread connecting a mom in Mbita, Kenya, to a mom in Denver, Colorado, is a thick cord of maternal instinct. Every mom wants good things for her child and to be the best mom she can be. Every mom wants her baby to grow up healthy and to have opportunities. Every mom has hopes and dreams for that perfect being she holds in her arms. The difference is the knowledge and resources that are available to her from the point at which she gives birth. How would a mom know that clean water is a crucial staple in the life of a healthy child if no one tells her? How could a mother dream that a simple schedule and hygiene routines will set up her child for educational success and a healthy life, unless someone shows her? How could she understand that the implications of investing in her own physical and emotional health are the two biggest predictors of her child's ongoing emotional and cognitive success?

The answers to these questions lie in our ability to develop and support the Lillians who are already out there around the world. They are sharp, instinctive women who, with just a bit of encouragement and simple resources, can change our future trajectory one mom at a time. They understand their culture and understand the discouraging roadblocks that moms face. They already have the prerequisite: a mom's heart and unfaltering belief that every mom matters and that even the smallest of support can make a better mom. And here is what we know for sure: Better moms make a better world, one child at a time.

Sherry Surratt is the president and CEO of MOPS International.

Chapter 19

Healthy Mothers Create Healthy Societies — and a Safer World

◄○► Kay Granger

Of the one billion people who live on less than $2 a day, a majority of them are women and girls. In less-developed countries, women and girls tend to be the most marginalized: Girls are less likely than boys to attend school. Many women routinely face violence and sexual attacks. And when it comes time to have kids, childbirth can mean life or death for many of these women.

Access to lifesaving maternal health care is one of the biggest challenges for women in the developing world. In fact, pregnancy is the leading cause of death for women ages fifteen to nineteen worldwide. Three years ago, I traveled to the Ayacucho region in Peru, 9,000 feet up in the Andes Mountains, to see these challenges firsthand. As a mother of three children, I felt an instant connection to the Peruvian mothers I met.

But their pregnancy experiences were far more dangerous than my own. In Ayacucho, women often deliver their children without clean delivery rooms or trained professionals. Throughout Peru, the country's maternal death rate has historically been unusually high. Mothers there are three times more likely to die while giving birth than in the United States.

When a mother dies, her children are less likely to eat well, go to school, and get immunized against diseases. Maternal and newborn deaths represent an estimated annual global financial loss of $15 billion in potential productivity.

After seeing this problem, the poverty-fighting organization CARE strengthened the community's capacity to address maternal health risks by convening a broad spectrum of health workers to develop practical emergency obstetric protocols and provide training and resources to implement them.

CARE also works with women and men to help them plan their families. For instance, CARE focuses on educating mothers in the community about spacing the births of her children and the benefits of doing so. When a woman plans the births of her children at least three years apart, she is less likely to suffer from delivery complications. Research has shown that improving such reproductive health services can also lead to gender equality and the reduction of poverty and social injustice.

As a result of these changes, women's lives in Peru were saved. There was a 50 percent reduction in maternal mortality in the area. During my visit, I met Isabel, a happy mother who had just given birth to twins. Because the community had worked with CARE to strengthen its maternal health systems for women, Isabel was able to get the care she needed from skilled workers and safely deliver her babies in a clean hospital.

Some may wonder why the issue of global women's health, particularly maternal health, should matter. The answer is simple: We live in a global community and are global citizens. We should all want to live in a world that supports the power and potential of women, no matter where they are. Providing an opportunity for women to be educated about maternal and reproductive health is the first step. Improvements in the lives of these women and countries help everyone, because progress and prosperity anywhere mean a more peaceful and stable world for us all.

Women around the world deserve to have healthy lives, healthy pregnancies, and healthy babies. Let's stand together with mothers around the world by lending our support for better global health services for women.

––––––––––––

Kay Granger represents the twelfth congressional district of Texas in the US House of Representatives.

Chapter 20

How I Became a Maternal Health Advocate

◄○► *Christy Turlington Burns*

The day I became a mother was also the day I became a maternal health advocate. After a healthy pregnancy and a birth that went exactly the way I'd hoped, I was unprepared for everything to change in a heartbeat. My placenta wouldn't detach, and I hemorrhaged. I didn't know it at the time, but this happens every day to women all over the world.

If you live in a country where skilled midwives and doctors are plentiful and you deliver in a well-staffed and stocked health care facility, as I did, then chances are you'll be fine. If you live in a country where most women deliver at home without a skilled attendant or in a facility where staff members don't have the skills or supplies to treat you, then you may join the ranks of the 287,000 women who die every year from entirely preventable or treatable complications. I was one of the lucky ones, and I realized I had been given a great opportunity to serve other women and make pregnancy and childbirth safe for every mother.

After my daughter's birth, I researched the multidimensional physical, social, economic, political, and cultural conditions that cause women to have poor maternal health. I learned that every two minutes, somewhere in the world, a mother dies from complications related to pregnancy and childbirth. I learned that in some parts of the world the main barrier is transportation, while in others it's lack of education, medications, or trained staff. In some cultures, women aren't allowed to seek medical care without permission, and in others they can't access family planning. I learned that child marriage, female genital mutilation, and teen pregnancy are all directly linked to maternal death and that when mothers die in childbirth, they leave, on average, four orphaned children. It was a steep learning curve that helped me decide the direction I wanted my advocacy to take.

I created a documentary, *No Woman, No Cry,* that highlighted the maternal health crisis from the perspectives of mothers and health care providers in four countries, including the United States. I wanted audiences to resonate with the fact that while 99 percent of maternal deaths occur in developing countries, 800 mothers per year die right here in America, where we rank sixtieth in the world for maternal mortality.

We need to make the health and lives of girls and women a priority.

The documentary was released in 2010 to audiences who were enthusiastic about helping find solutions. That's why I founded Every Mother Counts, a nonprofit organization focused on raising awareness about maternal health and mortality, funding grants that make a direct difference in improving maternal health and providing opportunities for people to get involved.

Currently, Every Mother Counts funds grants and projects in seven countries to address three main barriers that impact maternal health and health care everywhere—lack of transportation, education, and training, as well as supplies. We are addressing one or more of these gaps in Malawi, Uganda, Indonesia, Haiti, India, and the United States and will continue to identify and support programs that are designed to make services accessible to mothers around the world.

As daunting as the statistics are, we know that we already have the treatments, medications, and therapies necessary to prevent up to 98 percent of maternal deaths. We just need to make the health and lives of girls and women a priority. Every Mother Counts believes that together we can make pregnancy and childbirth safe for every mother.

Christy Turlington Burns is an advocate for maternal health. She is the founder of Every Mother Counts and the producer of No Woman, No Cry, a documentary about the problems of maternal health in the developing world.

Chapter 21

Family Planning and Linkages with US Health and Development Goals

A Focus on Ethiopia

◄◦► *Janet Fleischman*[1]

For decades, the United States has been the global leader in supporting voluntary family planning services around the world.[2] The benefits of family planning are numerous, not only for women's health, but also for increasing child survival, nutrition, education, and economic development, as well as preventing mother-to-child transmission of HIV. For these reasons, family planning is a core component of sustainable development.

On my recent visits to Ethiopia, I have seen firsthand some of the remarkable health and development progress attributed to increased access to family planning information and services around the country. According to the 2011 Demographic and Health Survey (DHS) in Ethiopia, the contraceptive prevalence rate almost doubled between 2005 and 2011, from 15 percent to 29 percent; a 2014 survey shows a further increase to 33.7.[3] The government's Health Extension Program (HEP) is

---

1. Janet Fleischman is a senior associate with the CSIS Global Health Policy Center. This article is adapted from the report she wrote with Alisha Kramer, "Family Planning and Linkages with U.S. Health and Development Goals: A Trip Report of the CSIS Delegation to Ethiopia," April 2014, http://csis.org/files/publication/140417_Fleischman_FamilyPlanningEthiopia_Web.pdf, and their November 2013 commentary, "Why Family Planning Is Central to Development," http://www.smartglobalhealth.org/blog/entry/why-family-planning-is-central-to-development/.

2. The President's budget request for FY2015 for US global health funding for global family planning/reproductive health is $538 million. See Henry J. Kaiser Family Foundation, "U.S. Global Health Funding: Family Planning/Reproductive Health (FP/RH), FY2001–FY2015," April 2014, http://kff.org/global-health-policy/slide/u-s-global-health-funding-global-family-planningreproductive-health-fprh/.

3. PMA2020, "PMA2014/Ethiopia: Performance, Monitoring & Accountability 2020," Johns Hopkins Bloomberg School of Public Health and Bill and Melinda Gates Institute for Population and Reproductive Health (January-March 2014), http://www.pma2020.org/sites/default/files/PMA2014Ethiopia_Round%20One_FP_Brief.pdf.

composed of 38,000 health extension workers (HEWs), almost entirely young women, who are trained, paid, and deployed around the country; the HEWs have contributed directly to rising awareness about the importance of delaying first births, healthy timing and spacing of pregnancies, and the availability of modern contraceptive methods. Another impressive result of the HEP has been the sharp reduction of under-5 child mortality, which has enabled Ethiopia to meet Millennium Development Goal 4. Much of this progress is due to the Ethiopian government's high-level commitment to health — especially family planning.

Yet Ethiopia faces daunting challenges. It is a vast, diverse country, with a population of 90 million, making it the second most populous country in Africa, and the population is projected to double by 2050. It is also one of the world's poorest countries, with limited resources to address a myriad of health, nutrition, and development problems. Maternal mortality remains stubbornly high,[4] due partly to the fact that only 10 percent of pregnant women deliver at health facilities. Unmet need for family planning also remains very high, especially among young women and married adolescents.[5] Cultural practices such as child marriage and female genital mutilation/cutting (FGM) put girls at escalated risk of adverse health outcomes when they begin to have children. Once pregnant, most of these girls will drop out of school, furthering their social isolation and limiting their opportunity to gain knowledge and skills that could empower them economically and socially. These challenges are compounded by the government's suspicion of civil society and the private sector; the government is especially restrictive in areas related to democracy and human rights. These factors complicate efforts to build sustainable family planning programs.

While support for international family planning has been a key feature

---

4. According to the UN Population Fund (UNFPA), maternal mortality in Ethiopia is estimated to be 350 per 100,000 live births, with estimates ranging from 210 to 630 per 100,000. See WHO, UNICEF, UNFPA, and The World Bank, *Trends in Maternal Mortality: 1990 to 2010* (Geneva: WHO, 2012), http://www.unfpa.org/ webdav/site/global/shared/documents/publications/2012/Trends_in_ maternal_mortality_A4-1.pdf.

5. According to UNICEF, between 2002 and 2012, 16.3 percent of girls in Ethiopia were married by the age of 15, and 47 percent were married by the age of 18. See UNICEF, "Ethiopia: Statistics" (December 2013), http://www.unicef.org/infobycountry/ethiopia_statistics.html.

of US global health policy, family planning has often been seen as contentious by some policymakers and other influential actors, particularly those who oppose abortion. These conflicts continue, even though US laws on foreign assistance clearly prohibit funding for abortion overseas.[6] Increasingly, however, ever-wider audiences, including many parts of the faith community and many who oppose abortion, have recognized the important goals of voluntary family planning, including healthy timing and spacing of pregnancies.[7] Ethiopia's progress helps to clarify and illuminate the value of family planning by learning from a dynamic national program.

US Health and Development Investments in Ethiopia

The United States has a complex bilateral relationship with Ethiopia, which includes important investments in the country's health and development programs, a significant peace and security relationship, and a complicated dialogue on democracy and human rights. On the health front, Ethiopia is a focus country for key US government health initiatives, including the President's Emergency Plan for AIDS Relief (PEPFAR) and the President's Malaria Initiative (PMI).[8]

---

6. The family planning and abortion restrictions included in the annual appropriations bills include: The *Helms Amendment* (1973): No foreign assistance funds may be used to pay for the performance of abortion as a method of family planning or to motivate or coerce any person to practice abortions. The *Tiahrt Amendment* (1998): Service providers or referral agents may not implement or be subject to numerical targets or quotas of total number of births, number of family planning acceptors, or acceptors of a particular family planning method; there may be no incentives, bribes, gratuities, or financial reward for family planning program personnel for achieving targets or quotas, or for individuals in exchange for becoming a family planning acceptor.

7. The U.S. Agency for International Development (USAID) requires that family planning programs comply with the principles of voluntarism and informed choice to ensure that women are free to choose whether to use family planning and, if so, what method is most appropriate for her; if a woman chooses sterilization, she must provide written voluntary and written consent. See USAID, "Voluntarism and Informed Choice," http://www.usaid.gov/what-we-do/global-health/family-planning/voluntarism-and-informed-choice.

8. For fiscal year 2013, 40 percent of USAID's budget in Ethiopia was focused on health: $37.1 million for maternal and child health (MCH), $30 million for family planning/reproductive health (FP/RH), $13 million for tuberculosis, $7.2 million for nutrition, and $43 million for malaria, totaling $130.3 million. New PEPFAR funding under Country Operational Plan (COP) 2013 will total approximately $271 million, including unexpended funds from previous fiscal years. This brings the US health budget to $401.3 million. Data from interviews with officials at the US Embassy in Addis Ababa, Ethiopia.

Ethiopia is also a major beneficiary of the Global Fund to Fight AIDS, Tuberculosis, and Malaria, to which the United States is the largest single donor. Given the Ethiopian government's focus on family planning and maternal health in its own health strategy, the United States is also a strong partner in those areas.

USAID in Ethiopia has focused on increasing utilization of family planning services through a number of approaches: building capacity of the HEWs to integrate family planning into community health and HIV/AIDS services; supporting scale-up of long-acting family planning methods, like implants and intrauterine devices (IUDs),[9] through the HEWs; strengthening private clinics to provide family planning/reproductive health services; providing contraceptive commodities and strengthening the logistics system; and supporting the Ministry of Health to improve monitoring and evaluation of the demand, uptake, and quality of family planning services.[10]

The Health Extension Program

The HEP is a hallmark of Ethiopia's health response. To remedy the fact that most health services were focused in urban areas, in 2003 the government launched an unprecedented program to bring basic primary and preventive health services to the entire country, including hard-to-reach rural areas. Health extension workers, almost entirely young women with at least a tenth-grade education, are selected from local communities; they are trained, paid by the government, and deployed back to their communities. The government's goal was to have two HEWs per *kebele*, the smallest administrative unit in Ethiopia, and to have the HEWs focus their efforts on health promotion activities, conducting house-to-house visits, and educating families about health and sanitation issues.

---

9. In fiscal year 2013, the US government procured over $9.7 million in contraceptive commodities for Ethiopia, including male condoms, Depo Provera, Microgynon, Jadelle, Implanon, and Combined Oral Contraceptives.

10. USAID Ethiopia presentation on MNCH and RH/FP Program to CSIS delegation (February 17, 2014).

From the start, family planning information and services have been key components of the HEWs' health package, and they demonstrated that providing more opportunities for services leads to escalating demand. Especially novel was the decision to allow the HEWs to deliver a range of family planning services; the HEWs have been trained to provide inject-able contraceptives (Depo-Provera) and to insert long-acting methods, such as the contraceptive implant Implanon, which remains effective for up to three years. Increasing access to family planning information through the HEWs is one of the ways that women and girls can protect their own health and that of their children. It also helps these women and girls to continue their education and increase their economic opportunities.

> **The important role of religious leaders in supporting family planning cannot be underestimated.**

In a rural health post in the Tigray Region, I spoke to a young woman named Mihret (see her story in Part 1), who has been a HEW for eight years and had received training through the USAID-funded Integrated Family Health Program implemented by Pathfinder International. She has seen many changes during that time, but remembers well the tough challenges at the outset. "Family planning was like a sin," she said. By gaining the support of local administrators and religious leaders, she finds that the community better understands the benefits of healthy timing and spacing. "If you get pregnant or married in school, you have to discontinue your education. Even if you can continue, having a child means you're not as active as the others.... It affects your achievement." Mihret herself was married at age twelve and had her first child at seventeen. "In my time, we didn't know where to get family planning," she said.

Engaging the Faith Community

The important role of religious leaders in supporting family planning cannot be underestimated. Ethiopia has a strong religious tradition, with the majority of the population belonging to the Eastern Orthodox Church (estimated at 43.5 percent), as well as a substantial

Muslim population (estimated at 33.9 percent) and Protestant denominations (18.6 percent).[11]

Faith leaders are very influential in shaping social norms in Ethiopia. Increasingly, many religious leaders are educating their followers about the dangers of harmful traditional practices such as early marriage; the importance of healthy timing and spacing of pregnancies; and HIV prevention and treatment. Although modern methods of contraception remain a sensitive topic for some religious leaders, concerted efforts to engage them about family planning and safe motherhood have been undertaken by health workers, nongovernmental organizations, and the government.

In some cases, the impact of these efforts is apparent in the changed attitudes of religious leaders. As one Orthodox priest told me, "Unknowingly, people say family planning is a sin. What is a sin is if you can't feed your children or send them to school." He continued, "From experience, we see that in families with limited children, they grow up well.... Women are physically stronger with spaced births."

This priest is part of a growing number of religious leaders who are speaking to their followers about family planning. At a health center down a narrow path from the main road, I met a deacon who worked as a family planning provider in a health center. "Women are happy when they hear I'm a deacon," he told me. "Women are afraid it will conflict with religious matters. I tell them there's no conflict, that they can use the service freely. I tell husbands that using family planning reduces children's and mother's health problems."

The deacon went on to describe the improvements in his community: many women have smaller families and are better able to care for their children. In addition, young married girls are not dropping out of school due to repeated pregnancies.

11. Central Intelligence Agency, "Africa: Ethiopia," *The World Factbook* (June 22, 2014), https://www.cia.gov/library/publications/the-world-factbook/geos/et.html.

Reaching Adolescents, Including Married Adolescents

Reaching adolescent girls with family planning information, especially married adolescents, remains extremely difficult. In the Amhara region, where the DHS found that almost 34 percent of girls age twenty to twenty-four had been married by the age of fifteen, I met many girls who had been married at ages twelve, thirteen, or fourteen and who were thirteen or fourteen at their first pregnancy. These girls described the barriers they faced in accessing family planning: husbands who refused to allow it, which left them no choice but to seek services secretly; mothers-in-law who found their pills and threw them out; and families and communities that saw no value in allowing them to stay in school.

These girls understood the possible health consequences of giving birth at such a young age. Sitting under a tree, a girl wrapped in a black scarf told me that she was fourteen when she experienced a prolonged and difficult labor: "I was not ready to give birth. My bones were not ready to give birth." Another girl told me about her friend who had been married at twelve and died in childbirth, and others described cases of fistula, resulting from giving birth at such a young age.

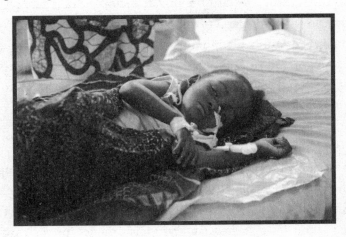

The girls I met were the fortunate ones. They had participated in unique programs, one organized by CARE and another by the Population

Council, designed to help married adolescents gain knowledge and skills, including information on health and family planning. As one of the girls explained: "Before the program, we followed the culture of our mothers — no child spacing. Year after year, we'd give birth. Now we understand the effect. We have a different understanding from our mothers."

The Challenges of Sustainability, Women's Empowerment, and Advancing US Policy

The Ethiopian government recognizes the value of incorporating family planning into its development agenda. Dr. Kesete Birhan Admasu, the Minister of Health, listed the ways that family planning has an impact on development, by allowing women to participate in microfinance and savings schemes, improving the nutritional status of their children, and enabling them to send their children to school. "Family planning isn't about limiting the family or population size," he told me. "It's about giving voice and choice to women in Ethiopia to decide when and whether to have children."

The important gains made in Ethiopia remain vulnerable. Despite increased financial commitments by the government, the public sector family planning program relies heavily on external funding. The government's uneasy attitude toward the private sector leaves a gap, given data that cost recovery and market segmentation could contribute to greater sustainability for family planning services. And while important changes have been registered in improving the status of women and girls, long-standing social and cultural barriers still impede equitable access to education, economic assets, and leadership positions.

Ethiopia shows that family planning is critical to advancing women's and children's health; it is also central to achieving broader US goals in health and development. Ethiopia's innovative HEP provides important lessons for other countries working to expand access to family planning and other basic health services. The United States should work with other interested countries to help adapt Ethiopia's model for their own context and to develop strategies to sustainably scale-up and finance such programs.

The successes in Ethiopia underscore the importance of continuing US global leadership in family planning. New opportunities for integrating family planning with other health and development priorities should be actively pursued and operationalized.

In the current US political environment, the challenge will be to expand areas of bipartisan common ground around family planning, to cultivate new champions across the political spectrum, and to advance linkages between family planning and other health and development goals. Ultimately, a woman's ability to decide when and whether to have children is directly linked to her ability to access economic empowerment opportunities, to educate and feed her children, and to keep herself and her family healthy — all goals that command wide support in the United States.

Family planning is inextricably intertwined with achieving broader health and development goals and should be a strategic priority for the United States. As Ethiopia's First Lady, Roman Tesfaye, told me, "To be engaged in the economic sphere, to create income, to contribute to family health and well-being and to the country's development, we must have family planning services."

Janet Fleischman is a senior associate with the Global Health Policy Center at the Center for Strategic and International Studies, where she focuses on women's health issues.

Chapter 22

Making Dreams Come True

◄◦► *Jennifer Nettles*

I am a planner. I prefer planning to surprises because I find so much joy in anticipating an event. So being a mother of "advanced maternal age" came with some perks for me. My American Medical Association specialists had machines so powerful that I could see the healthy flow of my child's blood throughout each chamber of his heart. I think those machines could have even given me a vision of him in his cap and gown graduating from college, if I'd asked for it.

The technology was truly amazing. So even though I can be a totally crunchy, granola, earth mama, you better believe we found out the gender of our baby as soon as was technologically possible!

It sounds romantically nostalgic to save the surprise of your baby's gender for his or her birth, but I had a feeling there could be *many* surprises on that day, so one more wasn't going to make or break the experience for us. Besides, I wanted to call my baby by name when I patted my very big belly and painted his room. I felt it was part of the prebirth bonding.

Of course, as expected, my birthing experience did come with its own set of surprises. I let Magnus take the reins on when he'd be born, to the tune of a week past his due date! Sheesh, buddy, get a move on! But an exhausting twenty hours later, my husband and I had a healthy, precious baby boy in our arms.

My experience in becoming a mother is an exceptional, first-world example. Justin and I were able to plan when we wanted to start our family. I was able to give birth with knowledgeable doctors to keep me healthy during my pregnancy and safe during my delivery. But sadly, many mothers across the world don't share in such a safe, joyous experience as they give life to their children.

Working with the Shalom Foundation of Nashville, Tennessee, has allowed me to witness closely the struggles of mothers and families in Guatemala. Guatemala is considered to be the second poorest country in the Western Hemisphere, right behind Haiti, and it is a land where extreme beauty is harshly shadowed by the extreme poverty of their people. And in this country, more than half of the population is under the age of eighteen. That takes a tremendous toll on the economy of a country.

For mothers in Guatemala, the experience of childbirth is vastly unlike mine. Only 36 percent of indigenous women give birth at a medical institution,[1] and many women who give birth at home do so without a trained birth attendant. Less than half of Guatemala's indigenous women have access to contraception, and these women living in extreme poverty are perhaps those who need it most, so they can choose to become pregnant only when they are ready to grow their families.

Can you imagine learning that you are pregnant, knowing that you can't afford to feed the children you already have? Or the desperation of facing difficult, possibly life-threatening pregnancy complications when you have children at home who depend on you for survival? My heart breaks for these women who have so little control over their lives, simply because access to resources is common in my everyday life.

---

1. Kanako Ishida, Paul Stupp, Reina Turcios-Ruiz, Daniel B. William, Evelyn Espinoza, "Ethnic Inequality in Guatemalan Women's Use of Modern Reproductive Health Care," *International Perspectives on Sexual and Reproductive Health* 38, no. 2 (June 2012): 99–108, http://www.guttmacher .org/pubs/journals/3809912.html.

The Shalom Foundation has stepped in, however, to help these beautiful children to be educated and to have access to medical resources to which they otherwise wouldn't. The foundation has built a school, where hundreds of children are being educated, and a medical facility that rivals that of the nicest hospitals in the area.

The result of this work is that hope is being cultivated in this community. As I sit with children and their mothers, I hear them dream of being teachers and singers and doctors. They dream of changing the world, making it a better place. I want to help make these dreams come true.

Jennifer Nettles is a Grammy-winning singer/songwriter, a performer, and an activist for women's and children's health in developing nations, specifically Guatemala. She and her husband live in Nashville, Tennessee, with their son.

Part 3

Other Concerns

◄○►

Male Involvement, Child Marriage,
Slavery, and Orphan Care

Namatta Lillian's Story
Uganda

My name is Namatta Lillian. I was born on a banana plantation in Uganda thirty-five years ago. Life as a young child was very difficult— horrible, even—because my father was a polygamist and had many wives and children. In our village, drinking was the customary activity at night. Men, girls, and elders would gather every night to drink alcohol until they became so drunk they would urinate on themselves, faint, or fight one another. To escape this activity, my siblings and I would play hide-and-seek or football, or we would help my mother with the domestic chores, which I enjoyed doing.

When I was nine years old, my father died of HIV/AIDS, and my mother took over the hard task of raising our big family by herself. She was not educated, so she worked by digging on farms, washing clothes, or collecting water. Still, she couldn't pay our school fees, and even eating two meals a day seemed like a miracle.

I stumbled in my education because it was very difficult for me to attend school every day due to the fees and the chores at home. I always felt out of place among my classmates, but I did dream of a life as a banker so that I could move away from this life of poverty.

When I was fifteen years old, I married. There was no ceremony; it was as if I just disappeared from my home and appeared at my husband's house. At first, my husband was kind and good to me, and he told me he loved me. But I became pregnant right away, and I was terrified seeing my stomach grow bigger every day. I thought abortion might be the best option for me, because I had no experience raising children. After my children were born, I was still so anxious and worried about tomorrow and how to care for them.

After about a year of marriage, my husband started drinking and smoking. He became hostile and started beating and kicking me at home. He refused to pay for food or rent for our family, and the owners eventually chased us from our rental house. There are so many misconceptions about women in Uganda; we are considered inferior, not allowed to make decisions about the home or to eat fine foods, like eggs, fish, chicken, or beef. Our culture has always dictated in favor of men.

But a friend told me about the benefits of family planning, and I now have nine children and have been able to use injectable birth control to be sure I don't have more. This gives me the opportunity to work by washing clothes or fetching water to help provide for my family.

Mothering here in Africa is by grace, love, and faith in God. Many times I wake up without food, medicine for my kids, and suffering daily abuse from my husband, yet as a mother nothing changes my passion and love for my children.

Kiran Awasthi's Story
India

My name is Kiran Awasthi, and I was born in a small village called Aata, situated in the eastern part of Kachauna Block, Hardoi District, Uttar Pradesh State, India. The people are poor and uneducated and depend on agriculture and daily labor for their livelihoods. There is no means of transportation or electricity.

My family consisted of six members—including three boys and me. I was the youngest child. My mother loved me very much, but I never heard my father express his affection during all my childhood. When I was old enough to understand, my mother told me my father went to jail when I was only two years old. My father stayed in jail for two years, and he died.

After my father's demise, our family migrated to a town called Chandigarh, where my uncle lived. I spent all my childhood days with my uncle, who was poor financially but rich at heart. We lived in a mud house, and every morning I went to work with my uncle at a merchant shop while my mother went to a construction site to earn our livelihood. Though I knew my uncle and mother loved me, as a girl child I lived my childhood in fear as I saw my older playmates being married off and realized that it could be my turn soon.

My three brothers started school when they were six years old; when I was six, no one talked about school for me. I thought that I might not get the chance to go to school, and I wanted to so much. Then one day my uncle announced that he was sending me to primary school. I was ecstatic! I attended on Monday through Saturday, 8:00 a.m. until 12:00 p.m. I took deep interest in my schoolwork and studied whenever I had free time.

Though coming from a poor family, I had high ambition and wanted to become a doctor and to heal my fellow poor villagers. When I was eleven years old, my brothers left our village to earn more money, but I stayed with my uncle and continued to go to school. My mother worked very hard, day and night, to support my education. After my primary education, I went to Chandigarh Government Inter-College and then went on to the actual government college in Chandigarh. There I completed my bachelor of arts degree, and I was gainfully employed.

I am thirty-three years old as I tell my story. I got married at age twenty when I was about to finish college. Though I wanted to continue my education and pursue my dream of becoming a doctor, I couldn't, due to limited financial resources. My uncle and mom wanted me to get married and settle down, and so did my in-laws. My marriage ceremony was celebrated with traditional dance and music, the Indian way, and was very nice, but like every girl, I wept when I left my mother and uncle's home.

My husband, Subhas Chandras Awasthi, was twenty-two years old when we got married. We have two children, a twelve-year-old boy and a nine-year-old girl. After my daughter was born, I used a method of family planning, and in March 2013 I opted for sterilization. My goal in life is to help my children fulfill their dreams.

I want the women of the United States to know that my uncle and mom have done me a great service by giving me an education. I was one of the fortunate women in rural India, and it has made a difference in my life. Basic education can fulfill a girl's dream. I went to school.

I know that education can change circumstances of many women's lives and that of her children in terms of healthy living, improving household income, and most importantly not thinking about where the next meal will come from. Giving us the opportunity to go to school is the way women in the United States can give us women in India hope and confidence to live our lives strong every day.

Chapter 23

What's So Scary About Smart Girls?

◄○► *Nicholas Kristof*

When terrorists in Nigeria organized a secret attack [in April 2014], they didn't target an army barracks, a police department, or a drone base. No, Boko Haram militants attacked what is even scarier to a fanatic: a girls' school.

That's what extremists do. They target educated girls, their worst nightmare.

That's why the Pakistani Taliban shot Malala Yousafzai in the head at age fifteen. That's why the Afghan Taliban throws acid on the faces of girls who dare to seek an education.

Why are fanatics so terrified of girls' education? Because there's no force more powerful to transform a society. The greatest threat to extremism isn't drones firing missiles, but girls reading books.

In that sense, Boko Haram was behaving perfectly rationally—albeit barbarically—when it kidnapped some of the brightest, most ambitious girls in the region and announced plans to sell them as slaves. If you want to mire a nation in backwardness, manacle your daughters.

What saddens me is that we in the West aren't acting as rationally. To fight militancy, we invest overwhelmingly in the military toolbox but not so much in the education toolbox that has a far better record at defeating militancy.

President Obama gives the green light to blow up terrorists with drones, but he neglects his 2008 campaign promise to establish a $2 billion global fund for education. I wish Republicans, instead of investigating him for chimerical scandals in Benghazi, Libya, would shine a light on his failure to follow through on that great idea.

So why does girls' education matter so much? First, because it changes demography.

One of the factors that correlates most strongly to instability is a youth bulge in a population. The more unemployed young men ages fifteen to twenty-four, the more upheaval.

One study found that for every 1 percentage point increase in the share of the population aged fifteen to twenty-four, the risk of civil war increases by 4 percent.

That means that curbing birthrates tends to lead to stability, and that's where educating girls comes in. You educate a boy, and he'll have fewer children, but it's a small effect. You educate a girl and, on average, she will have a significantly smaller family. One robust Nigeria study managed to tease out correlation from causation and found that for each additional year of primary school, a girl has 0.26 fewer children. So if we want to reduce the youth bulge a decade from now, educate girls today.

More broadly, girls' education can, in effect, almost double the formal labor force. It boosts the economy, raising living standards and promoting a virtuous cycle of development. Asia's economic boom was built by educating girls and moving them from the villages to far more productive work in the cities.

One example of the power of girls' education is Bangladesh, which until 1971 was (the seemingly hopeless) part of Pakistan. After Bangladesh gained independence, it emphasized education, including of girls; today, it actually has more girls in high school than boys. Those educated women became the backbone of Grameen Bank, development organizations like BRAC, and the garment industry.

Likewise, Oman in the 1960s was one of the most backward countries in the world, with no television, no diplomats, and radios banned. Not a single girl attended school in Oman. Then there was a coup, and the new government educated boys and girls alike.

Today, Oman is stable and incomparably better off than its neighbor, Yemen, where girls are still married off young and often denied an education. America is fighting Al Qaeda affiliates in Yemen and Pakistan with drones; maybe we should invest in girls' schools as Bangladesh and Oman did.

Girls' education is no silver bullet. Iran and Saudi Arabia have both educated girls but refused to empower them, so both remain mired in the past. But when a country educates and unleashes women, those educated women often become force multipliers for good.

Angeline Mugwendere was an impoverished Zimbabwean girl who was mocked by classmates because she traipsed to school barefoot in a torn dress with nothing underneath. She couldn't afford school supplies, so she would wash dishes for her teachers in hopes of being given a pen or paper in thanks.

Yet Angeline was brilliant. In the nationwide sixth-grade graduation examinations, she had the highest score in her entire district—indeed, one of the highest scores in the country. Yet she had no hope of attending seventh grade because she couldn't afford the fees.

That's when a nonprofit called the Campaign for Female Education, or Camfed, came along and helped pay for Angeline to stay in school. She did brilliantly in high school and is now the regional director for Camfed, in charge of helping impoverished girls get to school in four African countries. She's paying it forward.

Educating girls and empowering women are also tasks that are, by global standards, relatively doable. We spend billions of dollars on intelligence collection, counterterrorism, and military interventions, even though they have a quite mixed record. By comparison, educating girls is an underfunded cause even though it's more straightforward.

Readers often feel helpless, unable to make a difference. But it was a grassroots movement starting in Nigeria that grabbed attention and held leaders accountable to address it. Nigeria's leaders perhaps now realize that they must protect not only oil wells, but an even greater treasure: the nation's students.

Likewise, any of us can stick it to Boko Haram by helping to educate a girl. A forty-dollar gift at Camfed.org buys a uniform so that a girl can go to school.

We can also call on members of Congress to pass the International Violence Against Women Act, which would elevate the issue of sexual violence on the global agenda.

Boko Haram has a stronghold in northeastern Nigeria because it's an area where education is weak and women are marginalized. Some two-thirds of women in the region have had no formal education. Only 1 in 20 has completed high school. Half are married by age fifteen.

Obviously, the situation in the United States is incomparably better. But we have our own problems. It's estimated that 100,000 girls under eighteen years old in the United States are trafficked into commercial sex each year. So let's fight to #BringBackOurGirls in Nigeria but also here in the United States and around the world.

Nicholas Kristof is a journalist, author, op-ed writer, and winner of two Pulitzer prizes. This article was originally published in The New York Times, *May 10, 2014. Used by permission.*

Chapter 24

Men as Difference-Makers

◄○► *James Nardella*

Since 2009, I have been leading Safe Babies, an effort to bring health care to a rural population of mothers and infants in western Kenya. By building a rural hospital and mapping and tracking thousands of mother-baby pairs, we have been able to ensure that all pregnant women in our region deliver in the safety of a health facility, bring their newborns in for immunizations, and receive contraception to allow healthy spacing between pregnancies. Through these simple and effective steps, Safe Babies has reduced early infant mortality rates in our region by half.

Through this work I have learned the challenges women in a rural village face. As a male, I now better understand that the barriers to maternal and child health care are not only resource barriers (such as the need to build more maternity wards and provide ambulance services) or technical barriers (such as the need to train underskilled providers at health facilities), but also moral and gender barriers. So long as girls as young as thirteen are taken by men as brides, so long as schoolgirls are coerced by men into unwanted sex, so long as women are legally treated by men as property and valued only for their childbearing, and so long as male dominant practices such as polygamy, wife inheritance, and female genital mutilation exist, then our efforts to care for women and children must morally and culturally persuade men, not just financially and technically support women.

In these cultural and moral realms, the church has the power to influence men as family decision-makers and as difference-makers between life and death for the women and children in their village communities.

Let me put this in real terms through the story of a young mother I know in Kenya named Vivian.[1] The barriers Vivian has faced from her

---

1. All names in this story have been changed to protect individuals' identities.

husband in timing and spacing her pregnancies to protect her own health bring to light the complexity of the issue.

Vivian grew up near Lake Victoria, in a small rural village called Kadianga. Like many girls, she was unable to complete high school due to an unexpected pregnancy in eleventh grade. At seventeen, she became the wife of a man named Richard, who was six years older and a high school dropout himself. By the time Vivian was nineteen, she had a second child, and the family was surviving through subsistence farming.

One day in 2011, Vivian and her family plowed their field with the help of a neighbor's bull. That evening, as Vivian was leading the bull back to its owner, the animal charged her from behind and caught her with his horns, throwing her into the air. Vivian says that all she can remember was waking on the rocky ground and sensing the bull rushing at her again. As she was gored a second and third time, she screamed, and the neighbors came to her rescue, somehow managing to distract the bull and pull him away. The bull had badly wounded Vivian in the genital region, and she was rushed to the Lwala Community Hospital on the back of a motorbike.

At the hospital, clinicians cleaned, stitched, and dressed her wounds, but within a day, complications ensued and Vivian had to be transferred to a larger Catholic mission hospital for surgical repairs. As she was recovering in the Catholic hospital, doctors explained the imperative that Vivian delay future pregnancies until the wound could fully heal. They counseled her on family planning options, and she decided on an intrauterine device, a long-acting but reversible method.

However, upon being discharged from the hospital and returning home a week later, Richard forcibly removed the device, arguing that Vivian needed to bring him more children. Some days later, Vivian snuck away to the Lwala Community Hospital to request help in her situation. The clinicians talked her through other options, and Vivian elected to try a contraceptive implant, two tiny rods placed just under the skin in her inner arm.

By November 2012, Richard had become frustrated that his wife was not conceiving again. Vivian confessed to her husband that she was using contraceptives, and Richard became infuriated, threatening to cut the implant out of her arm himself. He forcibly brought Vivian back to the community hospital and demanded the implant be removed, holding his wife by the arm and screaming, "This is my property!" The clinical staff separated the couple and spoke privately with each spouse, explaining the importance of delaying any new pregnancies due to the injury. Without shame, Richard said, "I am the one to decide when she gives birth and when she needs family planning. If she comes home with this implant, I will beat her."

Despite this, Vivian had the courage to keep the implant, but within weeks the conflict at home had erupted again, and Vivian came back to request the removal of the implant, resigning by saying simply, "I want peace in my family." A short time later, Vivian conceived a third child. By the grace of God, the baby was born safely in 2013.

This is a story about culture and about values, not just health care. When women are valued primarily for their childbearing and treated as "beasts of burden," there are consequences for health, education, and the economy. There are moral and spiritual implications here for anyone who believes in a God of mercy and justice. Theologically, what does it mean for Vivian to be Richard's property? What does it mean for her freedoms to be restricted?

On the surface, this is the story of a controlling husband who lacks sympathy for a wife who has had a terrible injury, but through a lens of faith we see something more deeply true. I remember the way the encounter between Vivian and Richard played out in the hallway of our hospital and the disdain I felt toward Richard for his treatment of his wife. I was angry. But in a fallen world, each of us as men carry a bit of Richard in us—his broken view, his selfish attitude, and his narrow and untenable belief about the role of women. Maybe his behaviors and circumstance feel extreme, but we men are all Richards at some level by either what we have done or by what we have left undone.

Male leaders in the church are powerful vehicles for moral suasion in villages around the globe and possess the capacity to change the attitude and behavior of the Richards of this world. Male leaders in the church have the capacity to address the deep-seated prejudices that push Vivian from school, that value her only for her ability to bear children, that marry her off at a young age.

Vivian's challenge is not primarily accessing needed contraception. Her challenge is a lack of basic freedoms—to make decisions about her health, to have equal say in her family, to be protected from harm. The barriers to achieving these freedoms are holistic—gender-based violence, lack of education, teen pregnancy—so the solutions must be holistic as well.

Women like Vivian cannot negotiate these challenges and solutions alone. Men of conscience will need to stand up alongside women as advocates in local church communities and in global spheres of influence. As men we must be co-laborers in the effort to increase the freedoms women and children enjoy. As the Vivians of this world look for help in achieving healthy lives, in having the right to make decisions, what are we as men doing, and what are we leaving undone?

James Nardella is the executive director of the Lwala Community Alliance. He splits his time between Nashville, Tennessee, and East Africa.

Chapter 25

From the Shade of an Acacia Tree

Can Men Change?

◄○► *Dan Haseltine*

There are few areas of life where a man should feel as slippery footed as when he is discussing topics related to women. Men, historically, even with an abundance of resources — from tabloid magazine articles to physiological and psychological books — have been utterly confounded.

The task of writing about women is a scary one that I have put off until the very last minutes of my deadline. And so, in a book full of essays orchestrated to help us understand the role we play in serving vulnerable women and children around the world, I am going to attempt to stay out of the burning center of the discussion and stay closer to the shade trees on the fringe.

On a human level, which is where we should always be having this conversation, vulnerability is another way of saying we have a weakness. Perhaps we have a soft spot on our underbelly where our scales have fallen, where a marksman could inflict a devastating blow. As I see it, maybe our weakness is not our own skin but, rather, a part of our culture. Could a person's weakness, a woman's point of vulnerability, be another person?

If you have known any East African women, you would probably have difficulty finding any weakness or vulnerability in them. They are beautiful and strong, tenacious, creative, and courageous. My lexicon of glowing adjectives would run dry before I achieved the fullness of what the nearly goddess-like women of East Africa are like in my own eyes. I have watched them carry children and cinder blocks up mountains. I have watched them toil in the unforgiving sun, all the hours of the day, planting sugarcane and corn and then dancing the night away in joyous laughter.

I have experienced their leadership as they have forged the path to clean water and better health and hygiene for their children and families. Even in sickness, I have watched women mix concrete and build biosand filters for others in their villages. Have I hyped them enough?

You see, when I think about women and children in those communities of Africa, it is so hard for me to see them as vulnerable. At least, it is hard to consider their particular vulnerability to be something coming from within them, which brings me back to the shade on the fringe of the community. There are people in the shade we must consider.

If you have spent any time in Kenya or Rwanda or Zambia or Zimbabwe or Uganda, or any country in the developing west side of Africa, you have probably noticed that a lot of the men are like lions. They watch over the pride from the shade of the acacia tree.

The first time I set foot on African soil, it was obvious that there was a cultural understanding, different from the Western one I was accustomed to, regarding a man's place in the work of the community. In most of the villages I visited, I was greeted by women who were a part of leadership teams that established development plans for their communities. I realized early on that these women were the brawn *and* the brains of the operation.

We would gather under an old tree and drink warm orange Fanta and talk about why clean water and hygiene mattered to them. With the exception of a few elders, there were only ever a few men in the mix. I watched children carrying massive water jugs back and forth from the river. I watched women cutting sugarcane, tobacco, and maize while men lounged under trees, drank, and told stories to each other. In fact, the first time I carried water from a muddy watering hole, I was laughed at by a line of men who had come to observe the spectacle of a man carrying water. After all, only women and children did that.

Maybe it is old-fashioned, but there is something in the heart of a man that makes him feel like a failure if he is not able to provide for his family. I know that those men watching me that day had traveled a long way by foot, looking for employment. Looking but never finding. So I guess, if I reached, I could empathize with their story. The inability to provide is not just a Western form of emasculation. Economies fail. A man's vulnerable soul is preyed upon by circumstances he is unprepared to defend against. And sometimes the cultures that grow out of the frustration of failure become a problem, especially for women and children.

But the truth is, those same men who have no employment and who have lost a sense of direction play one of the most significant roles in the growth and health of their communities. The way men treat women always has a profound effect on the health and development of the world they live in.

Men have a role in the story of women who are deemed "vulnerable." Women are vulnerable to men who have grown up in a culture that does not value the sexual health of women and girls. Women are vulnerable to the men who perpetrate rape or who decide they do not want to wear a condom during intercourse. Women are vulnerable to men who do not have any cultural guardrails preventing them from sexually abusing children. Women are vulnerable to men who do not respect the bodies of women and believe women to be property. Women are vulnerable to men who act out their frustrations through sexual misconduct. Women are vulnerable to men who consider themselves superior to women.

I should not go much farther into this essay without acknowledging that not all men in Western Africa are like this. It would be a gross generalization to put all men in this category (however true it would be to imply that men, in general, have a bit of a superiority complex). That is for another conversation in another book.

So if there are cultural norms that perpetuate violence toward women, what role can men play in changing that culture? What role can we play in the support of women's health and safety? Perhaps it is not such a paradoxical idea that we could lead by serving.

Dan Haseltine is the lead singer of the band Jars of Clay and a co-founder of Blood:Water Mission, which aims to provide clean drinking water and HIV/AIDS treatments to people in underdeveloped parts of the world.

Chapter 26

Too Young to Wed
The Secret World of Child Brides

◄○► *Cynthia Gorney*

Because the wedding was illegal and a secret, except to the invited guests, and because marriage rites in Rajasthan are often conducted late at night, it was well into the afternoon before the three girl brides in this dry farm settlement in the north of India began to prepare themselves for their sacred vows. They squatted side by side on the dirt, a crowd of village women holding sari cloth around them as a makeshift curtain, and poured soapy water from a metal pan over their heads. Two of the brides, the sisters Radha and Gora, were fifteen and thirteen, old enough to understand what was happening. The third, their niece Rajani, was five. She wore a pink T-shirt with a butterfly design on the shoulder. A grown-up helped her pull it off to bathe.

The grooms were en route from their own village, many miles away. No one could afford an elephant or the lavishly saddled horses that would have been ceremonially correct for the grooms' entrance to the wedding, so they were coming by car and were expected to arrive high-spirited and drunk. The only local person to have met the grooms was the father of the two oldest girls, a slender gray-haired farmer with a straight back and a drooping mustache. This farmer, whom I will call Mr. M, was both proud and wary as he surveyed guests funneling up the rocky path toward the bright silks draped over poles for shade; he knew that if a nonbribable police officer found out what was under way, the wedding might be interrupted mid-ceremony, bringing criminal arrests and lingering shame to his family.

Rajani was Mr. M's granddaughter, the child of his oldest married daughter. She had round brown eyes, a broad little nose, and skin the color of milk chocolate. She lived with her grandparents. Her mother had moved to her husband's village, as rural married Indian women are expected to do, and this husband, Rajani's father, was rumored to be a drinker and a bad farmer. The villagers said it was the grandfather, Mr. M, who loved Rajani most; you could see this in the way he had arranged a groom for her from the respectable family into which her aunt Radha was also being married. This way she would not be lonely after her *gauna,* the Indian ceremony that marks the physical transfer of a bride from her childhood family to her husband's. When Indian girls are married as children, the gauna is supposed to take place after puberty, so Rajani would live for a few more years with her grandparents—and Mr. M had done well to protect this child in the meantime, the villagers said, by marking her publicly as married.

These were things we learned in a Rajasthan village during Akha Teej, a festival that takes place during the hottest months of spring, just before the monsoon rains, and that is considered an auspicious time for weddings. We stared miserably at the five-year-old Rajani as it became clear that the small girl in the T-shirt, padding around barefoot and holding the pink plastic sunglasses someone had given her, was also to be one of the midnight ceremony's brides.

The man who had led us to the village, a cousin to Mr. M, had advised us only that a wedding was planned for two teenage sisters. That in itself was risky to disclose, as in India girls may not legally marry before age eighteen. But the techniques used to encourage the overlooking of illegal weddings—neighborly conspiracy, appeals to family honor—are more easily managed when the betrothed girls have at least reached puberty. The littlest daughters tend to be added on discreetly, their names kept off the invitations, the unannounced second or third bride at their own weddings.

Rajani fell asleep before the ceremonials began. An uncle lifted her gently from her cot, hoisted her over one of his shoulders, and carried her in the moonlight toward the Hindu priest and the smoke of the sacred fire and the guests on plastic chairs and her future husband, a ten-year-old boy with a golden turban on his head.

◄ ◄◌► ►

The outsider's impulse toward child bride rescue scenarios can be overwhelming: Snatch up the girl, punch out the nearby adults, and run. Just make it stop. Above my desk, I have taped to the wall a photograph of Rajani on her wedding night. In the picture it's dusk, six hours before the marriage ceremony, and her face is turned toward the camera, her eyes wide and untroubled, with the beginnings of a smile.

I remember my own rescue fantasies roiling that night—not solely for Rajani, whom I could have slung over my own shoulder and carried away alone, but also for the thirteen- and the fifteen-year-old sisters who were being transferred like requisitioned goods, one family to another, because a group of adult males had arranged their futures for them.

The people who work full-time trying to prevent child marriage, and to improve women's lives in societies of rigid tradition, are the first to smack down the impertinent notion that anything about this endeavor is simple. Forced early marriage thrives to this day in many regions of the world—arranged by parents for their own children, often in defiance of national laws, and understood by whole communities as an appropriate way for a young woman to grow up when the alternatives, especially if they carry a risk of her losing her virginity to someone besides her husband, are unacceptable.

Child marriage spans continents, language, religion, caste. In India the girls will typically be attached to boys four or five years older; in Yemen, Afghanistan, and other countries with high early-marriage rates, the husbands may be young men or middle-aged widowers or abductors who rape first and claim their victims as wives afterward, as is the practice in certain regions of Ethiopia.

Some of these marriages are business transactions, barely adorned with additional rationale: a debt cleared in exchange for an eight-year-old bride; a family feud resolved by the delivery of a virginal twelve-year-old cousin. Those, when they happen to surface publicly, make for clear and outrage-inducing news fodder from great distances away. The 2008 drama of Nujood Ali, the ten-year-old Yemeni girl who found her way alone to an urban courthouse to request a divorce from the man in his thirties her father had forced her to marry, generated worldwide headlines and more recently a book, translated into thirty languages: *I Am Nujood, Age 10 and Divorced.*

But inside a few of the communities in which parent-arranged early marriage is common practice—amid the women of Rajani's settlement, for example, listening to the mournful sound of their songs to the bathing brides—it feels infinitely more difficult to isolate the nature of the wrongs being perpetrated against these girls. Their educations will be truncated not only by marriage, but also by rural school systems, which may offer a nearby school only through fifth grade; beyond that, there's the daily bus ride to town, amid crowded-in, predatory men.

The middle school at the end of the bus ride may have no private indoor bathroom in which an adolescent girl can attend to her sanitary needs. And schooling costs money, which a practical family is surely guarding most carefully for sons, with their more readily measurable worth. In India, where by long-standing practice most new wives leave home to move in with their husbands' families, the Hindi term *paraya dhan* refers to daughters still living with their own parents. Its literal meaning is "someone else's wealth."

Remember this too: The very idea that young women have a right to select their own partners—that choosing whom to marry and where to live ought to be personal decisions, based on love and individual will—is still regarded in some parts of the world as misguided foolishness. Throughout much of India, for example, a majority of marriages are still arranged by parents. Strong marriage is regarded as the union of two families, not two individuals. This calls for careful negotiation by multiple elders, it is believed, not by young people following transient impulses of the heart.

So in communities of pressing poverty, where nonvirgins are considered ruined for marriage and generations of ancestors have proceeded in exactly this fashion — where grandmothers and great-aunts are urging the marriages forward, in fact, insisting, I did it this way and so shall she — it's possible to see how the most dedicated anti-child-marriage campaigner might hesitate, trying to fathom where to begin.

"One of our workers had a father turn to him, in frustration," says Sreela Das Gupta, a New Delhi health specialist who previously worked for the International Center for Research on Women (ICRW), one of several global nonprofits working actively against early marriage. "This father said, 'If I am willing to get my daughter married late, will you take responsibility for her protection?' The worker came back to us and said, 'What am I supposed to tell him if she gets raped at fourteen?' These are questions we don't have answers to."

I heard the story of the rat and the elephant one day in early summer, some weeks into my time among girls who are expected to marry very young. I was in the backseat of a small car in remote western Yemen, traveling along with a man named Mohammed, who had offered to bring us to a particular village down the road.

"What happened in this village has given me strong feelings," he said. "There was a girl here. Ayesha is her name." The Prophet Muhammad's youngest wife was also named Ayesha, but this was not of interest to our Mohammed just now. He was extremely angry. "She is ten years old," he said. "Very tiny. The man she married is fifty years old, with a big belly, like so." Spreading his arm around him, he indicated massive girth. "Like a rat getting married to an elephant."

Mohammed described the arrangement called *shighar,* in which two men provide each other with new brides by exchanging female relatives. "These men married each other's daughters," Mohammed said. "If the ages had been proper between the husbands and new wives, I don't think anyone would have reported it. But girls should not marry when they are nine or ten. Maybe fifteen or sixteen."

Fifty families live in the rock and concrete houses of the village we visited, between cactus stands and dry furrowed farm plots. The local leader, or sheikh, was short and red-bearded, with a mobile phone jammed under his belt beside his traditional Yemeni dagger. He showed us to a low-ceilinged house crowded with women, babies, and girls. They sat on the carpeted floors and beds, and more kept ducking through the doorway to squeeze in; the sheikh squatted in their midst, frowning and interrupting. He regarded me dubiously. "You have children?" he asked.

Two, I said, and the sheikh looked dismayed. "Only two!" He tipped his head toward a young woman nursing a baby in one arm while fending off two small children with the other. "This young lady is twenty-six," he said. "She has had ten."

Her name was Suad. The sheikh was her father. She had been married at fourteen to a cousin he selected. "I liked him," Suad said, her voice low, as the sheikh kept his eyes upon her. "I was happy."

The sheikh made various pronouncements concerning marriage. He said no father ever forces his daughter to marry against her will. He said the medical dangers of early childbirth were greatly exaggerated. He said initiation to marriage was not necessarily easy, from the bride's point of view, but that it was pointless to become agitated about this. "Of course every girl gets scared the first night," the sheikh said. "She gets used to it. Life goes on."

His phone tootled. He extracted it from his belt and stepped outside. I pulled the scarf off my hair, something I'd seen my interpreter do when men were gone and the intimate talk of women was under way. Speaking quickly, we asked, "How are you all prepared for your wedding night? Are you taught what to expect?"

The women glanced toward the doorway, where the sheikh was absorbed in his phone call. They leaned forward. "The girls do not know," one said. "The men know, and they force them."

Could they tell us about young Ayesha and her elephant husband of fifty? The women all started talking at once: It was an awful thing; it should have been forbidden, but they were helpless to stop it. Little Ayesha screamed when she saw the man she was to marry, said a young woman named Fatima, who turned out to be Ayesha's older sister. Someone alerted the police, but Ayesha's father ordered her to put on high heels to look taller and a veil to hide her face. He warned that if he was sent to jail, he would kill Ayesha when he got out. The police left without troubling anyone, and at present—the women talked urgently and quietly now, because the sheikh appeared to be ending his conversation—Ayesha was living in a village two hours away, married.

"She has a mobile phone," Fatima said. "Every day, she calls me and cries."

"If there were any danger in early marriage, Allah would have forbidden it," a Yemeni member of parliament named Mohammed Al-Hamzi told me in the capital city of Sana'a one day. "Something that Allah himself did not forbid, we cannot forbid." Al-Hamzi, a religious conservative, is vigorously opposed to the legislative efforts in Yemen to prohibit marriage for girls below a certain age (seventeen, in a recent version), and so far those efforts have met with failure. Islam does not permit marital relations before a girl is physically ready, he said, but the Holy Koran contains no specific age restrictions and so these

> **The Holy Koran contains no specific age restrictions on marriage and so these matters are properly the province of family and religious guidance, not national law.**

matters are properly the province of family and religious guidance, not national law. Besides, there is the matter of the Prophet Muhammad's beloved Ayesha—nine years old, according to the conventional account, when the marriage was consummated.

Other Yemeni Muslims invoked for me the scholarly argument that Ayesha was actually older when she had marital relations—perhaps a teenager, perhaps twenty or more. In any case, her precise age is irrelevant, they would add firmly; any modern-day man demanding marriage with a young girl dishonors the faith. "In Islam, the human body is very valuable," said Najeeb Saeed Ghanem, chairman of the Yemeni Parliament's Health and Population Committee. "Like jewelry." He listed some of the medical consequences of forcing girls into sex and childbirth before they are physically mature: Ripped vaginal walls. Fistulas, the internal ruptures that can lead to lifelong incontinence. Girls in active labor to whom nurses must explain the mechanics of human reproduction. "The nurses start by asking, 'Do you know what's happening?'" a Sana'a pediatrician told me. "'Do you understand that this is a baby that has been growing inside of you?'"

Yemeni society has no tradition of candor about sex, even among educated mothers and daughters. The reality of these marriages — the murmured understanding that some parents truly are willing to deliver their girls to grown men — was rarely talked about openly until three years ago, when ten-year-old Nujood Ali suddenly became the most famous anti-child-marriage rebel in the world. Among Yemenis the great surprise in the Nujood story was not that Nujood's father had forced her to marry a man three times her age; nor that the man forced himself upon her the first night, despite supposed promises to wait until she was older, so that in the morning Nujood's new mother- and sister-in-law examined the bloodied sheet approvingly before lifting her from bed to give her a bath. No. Nothing in those details was especially remarkable. The surprise was that Nujood fought back.

"Her case was, you know, the stone that disturbed the water," says one of the Yemeni journalists who began writing about Nujood after she showed up alone one day in a courthouse in Sana'a. She had escaped her husband and come home. She had defied her father when he shouted at her that the family's honor depended on her fulfilling her wifely obligations. Her own mother was too cowed to intervene. It was her father's second wife who finally gave Nujood a blessing and taxi money and told her where to go, and when an astonished judge asked her what she was doing in the big city courthouse by herself, Nujood said she wanted a divorce.

A prominent female Yemeni attorney took up Nujood's case. News stories began appearing in English, first in Yemen and then internationally; both the headlines and Nujood herself were irresistible, and when she was finally granted her divorce, crowds in the Sana'a courthouse burst into applause. She was invited to the United States to be honored before more cheering audiences.

Everyone Nujood met was bowled over by her unnerving combination of gravity and poise. When I met her in a Sana'a newspaper office, she was wearing a third-grader-size black *abaya,* the full covering Yemeni women use in public after puberty. Even though she had now traveled across the Atlantic and back and been grilled by scores of inquisitive grown-ups, she was as sweet and direct as if my questions were brand-new to her. At lunch she snuggled in beside me as we sat on prayer mats and showed me how to dip my flat bread into the shared pot of stew. She said she was living at home again and attending school (her father, publicly excoriated, had grudgingly taken her back), and in her notebooks she was composing an open letter to Yemeni parents: "Don't let your children get married. You'll spoil their educations, and you'll spoil their childhoods if you let them get married so young."

Social change theory has a fancy label for individuals like Nujood Ali: "positive deviants," the single actors within a community who through some personal combination of circumstance and moxie are able to defy tradition and instead try something new, perhaps radically so. Amid the international campaigns against child marriage, positive deviants now include the occasional mother, father, grandmother, teacher, village health worker, and so on—but some of the toughest are the rebel girls themselves, each of their stories setting off new rebellions in its wake.

In Yemen I met twelve-year-old Reem, who obtained her divorce a few months after Nujood's; in doing so she won over a hostile judge who had insisted, memorably, that so young a bride is not yet mature enough to make a decision about divorce. In India I met the thirteen-year-old Sunil, who at eleven swore to her parents that she would refuse the groom who was about to arrive; if they tried force, she declared, she would denounce them to police and break her father's head. "She came to us for help," an admiring neighbor told me. "She said, 'I'm going to smash his head with a stone.'"

The push to reach many more underage girls and their families, through education programs and scattered government or agency-supported efforts, is targeted way beyond just the prepubescent marriages that most easily rouse public indignation. "The public loves those kinds of stories, where there's a clear right and wrong," says Saranga Jain, an adolescent-health specialist. "But the majority of girls getting married underage are thirteen to seventeen. We want to recharacterize the problem as not just about very young girls."

From the ICRW's point of view, *any* marriage of a teen under eighteen is a child marriage, and although definitive tallies are impossible, researchers estimate that every year 10 to 12 million girls in the developing world marry that young. Efforts to reduce this number are mindful of the varied forces pushing a teenager to marry and begin childbearing, thus killing her chances at more education and decent wages. Coercion doesn't always come in the form of domineering parents. Sometimes girls bail out on their childhoods because it's expected of them or because their communities have nothing else to offer.

What seems to work best, when marriage-delaying programs do take hold, is local incentive rather than castigation: direct inducements to keep girls in school, along with schools they can realistically attend. India trains village health workers called *sathins,* who monitor the well-being of area families; their duties include reminding villagers that child marriage is not only a crime, but also a profound harm to their daughters. It was a Rajasthan sathin, backed by the sathin's own enlightened in-laws, who persuaded the eleven-year-old Sunil's parents to give up the marriage plan and let her go back to school.

Because the impossible flaw in the grab-the-girl-and-run fantasy is: Then what? "If we separate a girl and isolate her from her community, what will her life be like?" asks Molly Melching, the founder of a Senegal-based organization called Tostan, which has won international respect for its promotion of community-led programs that motivate people to abandon child marriage and female genital cutting. Tostan workers encourage communities to make public declarations of the standards for their children, so that no one girl is singled out as different if not married young.

"You don't want to encourage girls to run away," Melching says. "The way you change social norms is not by fighting them or humiliating people and saying they're backward. We've seen that an entire community can choose very quickly to change. It's inspiring."

The one person who explained most eloquently to me the excruciating balance required to grow up both independent and respectful within a culture of early marriage was a seventeen-year-old Rajasthan girl named Shobha Choudhary. Shobha was in her school uniform, a dark pleated skirt with a tucked-in white blouse, the first time I met her. She had severe eyebrows, an erect bearing, and shiny black hair combed into a ponytail. She was in her final year of high school and a scholarly standout; in her village she had been spotted years earlier by the Veerni Project, which disperses workers throughout northern India in search of bright girls whose parents might let them leave home for a free education at its girls' boarding school in the city of Jodhpur.

Shobha is married and has been since she was eight. Picture the occasion: a group ceremony, a dozen village girls, great excitement in a place of great poverty. "Beautiful new clothes," Shobha told me, with a mirthless smile. "I didn't know the meaning of marriage. I was very happy."

Yes, she said, she had seen her young husband since the wedding. But only briefly. He is a few years older. So far she had managed to postpone the gauna, the transition to married life in his household. She looked away when I asked her impression of him and said, he is not educated. We regarded each other, and she shook her head; there was no possibility, none, that she would disgrace her parents by delaying the gauna forever: "I have to be with him. I'll make him study and understand things. But I will not leave him."

She wanted to go to college, she said. Her intense wish was to qualify for the Indian police force so she could specialize in enforcement of the child marriage prohibition law. She had been keeping a diary throughout high school. One of the entries read, in carefully lettered Hindi: "In front of my eyes, I'll *never ever* allow child marriages to happen. I'll save each and every girl."

Every time I visited Shobha's village, her parents served chai, or spiced tea, in their best cups, and the Shobha stories thickened in their layers of pride and dissembling and uneasiness as to what the foreign visitor was up to. It wasn't a wedding! It was only an engagement party! All right, it was a wedding, but that was before the Veerni people made their kind offer and Shobha's capability had astounded them all. It was Shobha who had figured out how to obtain electricity for the house, so that she and her younger siblings could study after dark. "I can sign things," Shobha's mother told me. "She taught me how to write my name." And now, her parents indicated, this fine episode was surely concluding—and it was time. The husband was calling Shobha's cell phone, demanding a date. Her grandmother wanted the gauna before old age overcame her.

The classes in Jodhpur were both Shobha's passion and her delaying tactic, but Veerni support runs only through high school; to stay on and cover the cost of college, Shobha needed a donor. The email arrived after I'd returned to the United States: "How are you I miss you Mam. Mam I am pursuing B.A. First year I also want to do English spoken course and computer course. Please reply mam fastly it is urgent for admission date in college."

My husband and I made the donation. "Let's see what happens,"

Shobha had said to me, the last time I saw her in India. "Whatever will be, I have to adjust. Because women have to sacrifice." We were in the cooking room of her family's home that afternoon, and my voice rose more than I intended: Why must women be the ones to sacrifice, I asked, and the look Shobha gave me suggested that only one of us, at that moment, understood the world in which she lives. "Because our country is man-oriented," she said.

She has completed more than a year now of post–high school study: computer training, preparation for the police exams. I receive emails from her occasionally—her English is halting but improving—and recently my Jodhpur Hindi interpreter borrowed a video camera and sat down with her, on my behalf, in a city café. Shobha said she was studying for the next exam. She had lodgings in a safe girls' hostel in the city. Her husband still called frequently. No gauna had yet taken place. She looked straight into the camera at one point, and in English, an enormous smile on her face, she said, "Nothing is impossible, Cynthia Mam. Everything is possible."

Two days after I received the video, a dispatch arrived from Yemen. Newspapers were reporting that a bride from a village had been dropped off at a Sana'a hospital four days after her wedding. Sexual intercourse appeared to have ruptured the girl's internal organs, hospital officials said. She had bled to death. She was thirteen years old.

Cynthia Gorney is a professor of journalism at University of California, Berkley. This article was originally published in National Geographic *magazine, June 2011. Used by permission.*

Chapter 27

Child Marriage and Dowry Deaths

◄○► *Jimmy Carter*

Another serious and pervasive example of gender abuse is the marriage of young girls, often without their consent and contrary to their best interests.

There are an estimated 14 million girls married every year before they reach the age of eighteen, and 1 in 9 of these are younger than fifteen. This includes 48 percent of young brides in South Asia; 42 percent in Sub-Saharan Africa; 29 percent in Latin America and the Caribbean; and 18 percent in the Middle East and North Africa. Girls from poor families are nearly twice as likely to be married at an early age as girls from wealthier families.

This is a traditional practice in many societies, primarily because girls are not considered equal in value to boys and are often believed to be a burden to their family. When poverty is a factor, marrying off a daughter is a convenient way to eliminate the need to feed her. Another financial incentive is the "bride price" paid to the girl's family.

A traditional practice that has become subject to serious abuse is the payment of a dowry by the bride's family. Especially in India and Pakistan and their neighbors it has become more prevalent in recent years, and the amount paid has also increased. Recognizing this burden, especially on poor families, India and other countries have outlawed the practice, but the law is widely ignored, even among the more affluent families. Since girls are considered to be a burden on the family and unmarried ones an embarrassment, many families are willing to go bankrupt to get them married. As a result, thousands of young women suffer.

In January 2012, the *Times of India* reported an increase in the killing of brides by greedy husbands and in-laws when they don't receive enough money and jewelry from the bride's parents, or in lieu of returning unsatisfactory brides (along with the dowry) to their parents. This terrible crime is called "dowry death," and women's organizations in India have increased pressure for more stringent laws against it. In 1986 a law was passed against murder resulting from harassment for dowry, with a section added later to define more specifically the crimes of harassment and cruelty by the husbands and their families.

However, these stricter laws have had little effect: when cases are actually brought to trial, conviction rates have dropped. In 2000, 6,995 dowry deaths were reported under these new laws; in 2010, 94,000 cases were reported, with a conviction rate of just 19 percent; in 2012 the number of cases fell to 8,233. There is no data yet available for the conviction rate.

There are proven disadvantages for child brides concerning their health, education, safety, and loss of the basic human right of making decisions about their own lives. Young brides under fifteen are five times more likely to die in childbirth than women in their twenties, and when a woman is under eighteen, her baby is 60 percent more likely to die in its first year of life than a baby born to a woman just two years older.

Few child brides are permitted to remain in school, which deprives them of the ability to support themselves or a family. In addition, they are more likely to suffer domestic violence and sexual abuse. All these statistics are derived from publications of the United Nations agencies. This mistreatment contravenes both the Convention on the Rights of the Child and the Convention on the Elimination of All Forms of Discrimination Against Women.

If the abuses of child marriage continue at the present rate, then about 15 million girls will be added each year to the list of victims. This terrible situation has been ignored by most of the international community, largely because the young girls are inarticulate, their families have a selfish financial interest, and political leaders consider the prohibition of forced child marriage a taboo issue, since it is supported by traditional and religious culture.

I am a member of The Elders, a group of former political leaders, peace activists, and human rights advocates who were brought together by Nelson Mandela in 2007. The goal Mandela set for us was to use our "almost 1,000 years of collective experience" to work on solutions for problems involving peace, human rights, climate change, and disease. One of the criteria we adopted is to be free of political pressures by not holding public office, but all of us have had experience in high positions.[1]

The Elders have been active in attempts to promote peace and human rights in the Middle East, Sudan and South Sudan, Zimbabwe, Cyprus, Kenya, Egypt, North and South Korea, and Myanmar and in addressing the impending disaster of global warming. But one of our most challenging and exciting commitments has been to promote equality for women and girls.

---

1. The Elders are Martii Ahtisaari, president of Finland, Nobel Peace laureate; Kofi Annan, secretary-general of the United Nations, Nobel Peace laureate; Ela Bhatt, founder of the Self-Employed Women's Association of India; Lakhdar Brahimi, foreign minister of Algeria and United Nations envoy; Gro Harlem Brundtland, prime minister of Norway and director general of the World Health Organization; Fernando Henrique Cardoso, president of Brazil; Jimmy Carter, president of the United States, Nobel Peace laureate; Hina Jilani, Pakistani lawyer and UN special representative on human rights defenders; Graça Machel, education minister of Mozambique and widow of Nelson Mandela; Mary Robinson, president of Ireland and United Nations high commissioner for human rights; and Ernesto Zedillo, president of Mexico.

We had an extensive debate when I presented my concerns about the adverse impact of religious beliefs on women's rights to this group of fellow leaders and advisors in 2008, because they represent practicing Protestants, Catholics, Jews, Muslims, and Hindus, and their faiths have different policies about the status of women. We finally decided to draw particular attention to the role of religious and traditional leaders in obstructing the campaign for equality and human rights and promulgated the following statement:

> The justification of discrimination against women and girls on grounds of religion or tradition, as if it were prescribed by a Higher Authority, is unacceptable. Having served as local, state, national, and world leaders, we understand why many public officials can be reluctant to question ancient religious and traditional premises — an arena of great power and sensitivity. We are calling on all those with influence to challenge and change the harmful teachings and practices — in religious and secular life — that justify discrimination against women, and to acknowledge and emphasize the positive messages of equality and human dignity.

After The Elders agreed to adopt the eradication of gender abuse as a priority project in 2008, it soon became obvious that the greatest opportunity for our group to make a direct and immediate contribution was by concentrating on child marriage. The Elders formed a global partnership with about 300 nongovernmental organizations [NGOs] from more than fifty countries that share the commitment to end child marriage. We named this coalition Girls Not Brides, and it grew to such an extent that it was separated into an independent organization in 2013, with The Elders still fully supportive of its goals.

All the NGO partners are continuing work in their own areas, and substantial progress is being made in raising international concern about the issue. Plans have been announced to raise the subject with the UN Human Rights Council, with the goal of reaching a General Assembly resolution condemning the practice.

In the meantime, other action is being taken. In 2013 Human Rights Watch released a ninety-five-page report on South Sudan that documents the near total lack of protection for girls and women who try to resist marriage or leave abusive marriages and the obstacles they face in achieving any relief from their plight. The US Congress has passed a law that requires the inclusion of child marriages in its annual Human Rights Report and mandates that the secretary of state develop a strategy to prevent child marriage, including diplomatic and program initiatives. Both the United Nations and the World Bank have announced commitments to publicize the problem and to induce nations to end the practice.

There are many encouraging developments; one is a special effort to assess the links between child marriage and slavery and to sharpen national and local laws so they are more specific and punitive when girls are forced to act against their will. Despite the persistence of the practice in many communities, these efforts have had some tangible benefits. In ninety-two countries surveyed in 2005, 48 percent of women forty-five to forty-nine years old were married as children, but the proportion is only 35 percent for women who are now twenty to twenty-four. The trend is good news, but the number is still far too high!

Jimmy Carter is the former President of the United States of America and the winner of the 2002 Nobel Peace Prize. Taken from A Call to Action *by Jimmy Carter (New York: Simon & Schuster, 2014). Used by permission.*

Chapter 28

A Promise to Girls

◄○► *Desmond Tutu and Ela Bhatt*

This day [the first-ever International Day of the Girl, October 11, 2012] is a day to celebrate the fact that it is girls who will change the world; that the empowerment of girls holds the key to development and security for families, communities, and societies worldwide. It also recognizes the discrimination and violence that girls disproportionately endure—and it is especially important that one of the cruelest hardships to befall girls, child marriage, should be the United Nations' chosen theme for this inaugural day.

The marriage of adolescent girls, sometimes to much older men, sums up much of the harm, injustice, and stolen potential that afflict so many girls around the world.

Ten million girls under the age of eighteen are married off, every year, with little or no say in the matter.

◄○►

Imagine the wonderful force we would unleash if these girls could be spared such a life.

◄○►

That's 100 million girls in the next decade. Their parents may feel they are doing the right thing to protect their daughters, but in reality these brides will be vulnerable to ill health, violence, inadequate education and poverty—as will their children.

Unlocking Girls' Potential

Imagine, instead, the wonderful force we would unleash if these girls could be spared such a life.

They would be more likely to stay in school. Studies have shown that when girls stay longer in primary school, they earn wages up to 10 to 20 percent higher in their adult lives. As they get older, the differences in earnings are even more encouraging: for every extra year in secondary school, they can earn up to 25 percent more in adulthood.

These girls would also be more likely to be healthy and less likely to contract diseases such as HIV/AIDS than married girls of the same age. And when a woman does eventually start a family, again experts have shown the benefit of having enjoyed a healthy, educated, and safe childhood: rates of maternal and child mortality are also improved by better education, while there are also likely to be happier relations between husband and wife and within the family. What is more, women reinvest more money into their family than men do—so everyone benefits from the higher earnings.

And we know, having seen it firsthand in successful efforts to reduce child marriage, that these women won't let their daughters marry as children. Child marriage could cease to exist with their generation.

Today we have the opportunity to enshrine such a global pledge to end child marriage.

Child Marriage Hinders MDGs

The Millennium Development Goals (MDGs), international targets set at the turn of the century, proved it was possible to think, and to act, on the largest of scales: halving extreme poverty, halting the spread of HIV/AIDS, and providing universal primary education are some of its objectives, all by the target date of 2015. Unlike many international commitments, the MDGs are still remembered years later and helped galvanize unprecedented efforts by governments.

Important progress has been made toward meeting the MDGs: For instance, the target of halving the proportion of people without reliable access to improved drinking water has already been met, and primary school enrollment of girls has equaled that of boys. Overall the MDGs have made a historic contribution toward reducing poverty.

But this progress will be stunted if we fail to address injustices as staggering, persistent, and widespread as child marriage. As our leaders begin the process of preparing new development goals to succeed the MDGs, the persistence of child marriage should be seen as one of the major barriers to the well-being of our human family.

Challenging Traditions Through a Global Partnership

Too often, child marriage is justified on the basis of custom or tradition. While traditions often serve to bind societies together, we also want to point out that traditions are man-made. If we learn that they are harmful, we should change them.

In our travels, as Elders, in Asia and Africa, we have met brave girls—and boys—who do not hesitate to stand up to tradition and say no to child marriage. In Bihar, a state in northeast India where nearly 70 percent of girls marry before they turn eighteen (contrary to national law), we met admirable young people who were signing pledges not to marry before eighteen. In Amhara, a region in northern Ethiopia, where the most common age for a girl to marry is twelve, we visited girls who participated in workshops to discuss collectively the benefits of ending child marriage.

These meetings have convinced us that there is a real need to connect groups around the world, enable them to work together, and help to end this practice for the benefit of us all. This led to the creation of Girls Not Brides, a global partnership of organizations dedicated to stopping the practice, with a membership now growing in the hundreds.

Day after day, the voices of these girls and boys continue to rise higher up the international agenda. We believe that an international consensus on the need to end child marriage is within sight.

When we created Girls Not Brides in 2011, we committed to ending child marriage in one generation. Why not, then, pledge the elimination of this harmful practice by 2030?

Development targets to improve global health, education, and gender equality would also be directly tackled by a pledge to end this devastating practice.

And generation after generation, girls would be able to fulfill their potential, amplify the benefits bestowed upon them by their own mothers—and bless their daughters to do the same.

On this inaugural Day of the Girl, we call on the international community to promise a different life to those girls — a life of their choosing.

Ela Bhatt founded the Self-Employed Women's Association, now one of India's biggest trade unions with more than 1.2 million members. Desmond Tutu is archbishop emeritus of Cape Town and a Nobel Peace Prize laureate. They are members of The Elders, a group of independent leaders working for peace, justice, and human rights. This piece was published in newspapers around the world for the first International Day of the Girl on October 11, 2012. Used by permission of The Elders.

Chapter 29

Forced to Confront the Impossible

◄○► *Christine Caine*

I recall a story of a young teen girl we will call Sari. She sat perched quietly on a chair. The sun was setting outside the brothel in a small town on Thailand's border with Malaysia. Sari's long hair hung forward, shielding her face from view. The eldest of four children, with two disabled parents, she was from a small, poor hill-tribe area in Laos.

The conversation progressed slowly, interrupted with long pauses as our team gently found a way to communicate in a culture where women and children are seen but not heard. The gulf between our team and Sari was bridged by our desire to understand the unimaginable and Sari's desire to give voice to the unspeakable: a young girl of probably no more than fourteen years old, whose mother had sold her to a brothel. We had been steeped in our antislavery work in Eastern Europe, where girls were promised work as waitresses but tricked and forced into brothels, but the answers Sari bravely gave stopped us in our tracks. We came to realize that an entire culture is aware and even complicit in modern-day slavery.

We asked Sari whether she had known the nature of the work involved. We asked if she knew when she left her family to travel to Thailand that her evenings would be spent in a brothel, sexually servicing men many times a day. We asked if she knew she would be living in a crammed room with as many as ten girls, sleeping all day to work all night. We asked if she knew that the town she would live in would be a modern-day Sodom and Gomorrah, with over 140 brothels to fill the small town.

Lifting her right hand to fiddle with her long hair, she slowly raised her eyes to meet ours: "Yes," she said, "I knew. I knew what I would be doing when I got here. My mother told me." A pregnant pause followed, while the import of her words overtook our team seated in the room. "My mother said it was my decision — my decision whether I came ... or not."

As we continued to sit in stunned silence, Sari then rose to leave as she explained it was time for her to "work." Smiling through her tears, she stopped in the doorway and looked back, striving to clarify for us the incomprehensible: that while she was a fourteen-year-old, heartbroken to be doing this work, she was happy that the money her trafficker sent back to her family in Laos put food on the table for her parents and siblings.

> **When we look at the greatest liberator of history, Jesus, we see he welcomed and esteemed the marginalized and mistreated — the women and children.**

The issue of maternal-child health in developing countries like Laos and Thailand, where the A21 Campaign combats sex slavery, is a pressing topic. Staged against the backdrop of desperate women without education — poor, hungry, and surrounded by more mouths than they can feed — rises the fastest-growing criminal economy in the world: human trafficking. Put simply, human trafficking is modern-day slavery. As the second largest criminal economy on the planet, trafficking generates over $32 billion per year, brokered on the backs of young girls like Sari.

Unfortunately, the variables of human trafficking and societies that routinely mistreat women collide in developing nations to create a perfect storm that leads to horrifying results: (1) these women exist in rural villages with no income-generating opportunities; (2) these women know their children will die or minimally fail to thrive for lack of basic necessities; (3) the problem is solvable by ripping apart the sanctity of the maternal-child bond and agreeing to sexually commoditize and enslave the eldest daughter, selling her to the only industry in town that generates any money: the sex-trafficking industry.

No woman should be forced to confront the impossible: selling one child to ensure survival of the rest. We must advocate and educate so that young girls will no longer be faced with Sari's choice of watching siblings starve or "choosing" instead to sexually service men three times their age.

In the midst of this very dark, daunting circumstance, there is a ray of hope. *We* can do something. *You* can do something. We can effect change for these girls, and for generations of girls to come, by supporting maternal and child health and healthy timing and spacing of pregnancies. For young girls like Sari, already imprisoned by human trafficking, this knowledge can empower her to protect herself and her body, and it can offer her a hope that there may be a future free from the sex trade.

We must elevate the status of women and children in developing countries. When we look at the greatest liberator of history, Jesus, we see he welcomed and esteemed the marginalized and mistreated—the women and children. In the economy of God, our value is priceless. We—human beings made in the image of God—are not commodities. Valued, loved, honored, and priceless, when we educate and elevate the status of the oppressed, a difference is made.

As Christians, we know that children like Sari are not commodities and that the parental bond between mother and child is meant to be cast in the image of Jesus' love for us. As Psalm 127:3 reminds us, children are neither tools nor a means to an end, but our very future, both a *gift from our Lord* and *a reward from him*. Put simply, educating and esteeming women is not a luxury in the countries in which the A21 Campaign works, but a necessity—a key that will allow parents to move from forced commoditization of their children to treating them with the unconditional love Jesus bestowed in Matthew 19:13–15 (NLT):

> Some children were brought to Jesus so he could lay his hands on them and pray for them. The disciples told them not to bother him.

> But Jesus said: "Let the children come to me. Don't stop them! For the Kingdom of Heaven belongs to such as these."

> And he put his hands on their heads, and blessed them before he left.

Christine Caine is director of Equip and Empower Ministries and co-founder of the anti-human trafficking organization the A21 Campaign. She is author of Undaunted: Daring to Do What God Calls You to Do. *Christine and her husband, Nick, live with their two daughters in California.*

Chapter 30

Brothels, Survival, and Hope

◄○► *Natalie Grant*

It was Enya's[1] twelfth birthday, and her parents had planned a special trip. Although her remote Indian village was only four hours outside of the bustling city of Mumbai, she had never been there but had dreamed of seeing its bright lights and busy streets. On her twelfth birthday, her parents were making her dream a reality.

As the overly crowded train pulled into the station in downtown Mumbai, Enya was overwhelmed by the sights, smells, and sounds. But as the mass of humanity began to exit the train, her hand slipped out of her father's. She turned and looked but couldn't find her father or mother. Believing she would spot her parents as soon as the crowd cleared, an anxious Enya made her way off the train and waited in the station. Yet, as the crowd dissipated, she still could not find her parents.

Enya was lost and alone, until a man approached her and told her that he and his wife would give her a meal and help her find her mom and dad. But twelve-year-old Enya would soon learn there was no wife, no meal, and no reunion with her parents. There was the trunk of a car, then a dirty floor, where she would be exploited and abused over fifteen times in her first twenty-four hours of captivity. Enya's parents had sold her. They believed she would receive an education and have the chance of a better life in exchange for light housework. Instead, she was a victim of human trafficking and forced to be a sex worker for the next eight years of her life.

Every day, around the world, millions of children are exploited through modern-day slavery. Human trafficking is the fastest-growing criminal enterprise in the world, following drug trafficking in total profits, which it is expected to pass in the near future. From factory workers in Bangladesh to brothels in Cambodia and Thailand, children are used to provide

---

1. Names have been changed to protect victims' identities.

services from sewing to sex. The actual number of exploited children is unknown, but we know that factors such as lack of education, poverty, and desperation lend to the problem.

After becoming aware of the reality of modern-day slavery and the commercial exploitation of children, I traveled to India and came face-to-face with the evil of sex trafficking for the first time. There I met children as young as six who were being exploited in the sex trade. It was during this trip that I met Enya and heard her story—sold by her own parents, who were driven by poverty and desperation. And yet, despite the fact that this child had been sold into slavery by those she trusted most, Enya had longed to see them and let them know that she was safe and doing well.

This episode illustrates the interface between maternal health, family planning, and child trafficking. According to Jeff Barrows, MD, director of advocacy and education at Hope for Justice (formerly Abolition International), children arising from unplanned pregnancies are at far greater risk of trafficking. This twelve-year-old girl was sold into slavery because her parents could no longer provide for her. While poverty increases the risk of child trafficking, it also increases the risk of unplanned pregnancies due to the lack of access to reliable forms of contraception. As an ob-gyn physician and anti-trafficking advocate, Dr. Barrows is aware that family planning does reduce unplanned pregnancy and thus prevent certain cases of child trafficking.

Many of the children I saw struggled with life-threatening illnesses such as HIV/AIDS, and I was told by anti-trafficking workers in the field that in many impoverished villages there are almost no children over the age of ten. They are sent to work in either fields, factories, or brothels, believing that the "opportunity" will help secure a better future for their families. I personally saw ropes tied to the bedposts in brothels, where women tethered their small children so that they would not crawl away while their mothers worked servicing clients.

Still in other areas, such as Moldova in Eastern Europe, many children are abandoned when their parents leave to work abroad. Over 80 percent of Moldovans leave the area to find work because of limited opportunities at home, thus leaving their children in the care of orphanage personnel.

This issue creates vulnerable children who age out of the orphanages and are desperate to find ways to support themselves. Many of these young teens are tricked to believe they are being sent to work in retail or attend university, only to learn later that they've been duped into working in the sex trade. It is important to emphasize that family planning can help parents have only the children they can afford and reduce the risk of having to abandon those children into orphanages.

I have sat with many victims, both from faraway places to here in the United States, who have been exploited as a result of abuse and neglect often stemming from poverty. In many cases, their families are also caught in the same vicious cycle, willing to do whatever it takes to survive. Oftentimes, their mothers are victims themselves, and some of the children are born out of unfortunate circumstances. Every victim desires reconciliation and love, the opportunity for healing, acceptance, and success, regardless of their circumstances.

One of the critical issues facing girls victimized in the commercial sex trade is the betrayal of parents or family members and the journey toward reconciling the idea of family against the horrible trauma suffered in their exploitation. James Pond, one of our directors and an expert on sex trafficking and survivor aftercare, says,

> Poverty and family planning are an important factor in the trafficking of young girls in Southeast Asia. The value of a single child is not in

question; rather, the potential for exploitation of a child for a family experiencing desperation or other extenuating circumstances around poverty directly impact the likelihood of abuse. With better options around family planning and other intervention strategies, we have the opportunity to save thousands of young lives from the horror of trafficking, exploitation, and abuse.

As a mother myself, I understand the relationship between mother and child. The bond between a mother and her child is one of the most powerful connections that exist. Most of us could not imagine ever making a choice that would cause harm to our children, but to thousands around the world, this nightmare is a reality. For many around the globe, the lack of educational programs, access to medical resources such as contraception and healthy lifestyle choices, overwhelming poverty, and violence drive mothers to situations where they have no options.

With more resources in impoverished areas, we could provide opportunities that would lead to life-altering options outside of slavery and exploitation. My hope is that more people — professionals and laypeople — will link arms, develop materials that will lead to change, and give thousands a chance for a hope and a future.

Natalie Grant is a multiple Dove Award-winning, Grammy-nominated singer-songwriter and the founder of Hope for Justice (formerly Abolition International), a nonprofit organization dedicated to eradicating sex trafficking.

Chapter 31

Contraceptives in the Developing World

A Focus on Haiti

◄○► *Tony Campolo*

You may have heard about the *restaveks* of Haiti. Technically, they are not slaves, but they might as well be. They are children who have been given away by their mothers, who, because of their poverty, were unable to adequately care for them.

Imagine a mother living in a somewhat isolated mountain village, who already has more children than she can feed, who suddenly has to deal with an unwanted pregnancy. In her despair she is very vulnerable to promises made by an enterprising entrepreneur who tells her that he is able to find a much better-off family who will feed, clothe, and educate one of her children. To her, this really is a chance to give one child a life with a hopeful future, beyond anything that she could expect to offer.

This is usually how a child becomes a *restavek*, which in the Creole vocabulary of Haiti means "a live-in." That is how this mother's eleven-year-old daughter is given away and is soon placed with a family in the big city of Port-au-Prince.

Sadly, there is a slight likelihood that any of what was promised will be delivered, and in most cases there is extreme disappointment. The strong probability is that this vulnerable eleven-year-old girl will never get to go to school as promised, but will spend her days cleaning, running errands, carrying buckets of water, cooking, and serving meals to the family that "bought" her from that enterprising, immoral entrepreneur. After the evening meal, if there are any scraps of food left over, she might get something to eat. If she complains, she is likely to be beaten—the least of the sufferings she might endure. As she gets older, sexual molestation could be her lot.

There may be as many as 200,000 *restaveks* in Haiti, and their stories are sad replications of the one I just told you.

When the earthquake hit Port-au-Prince in 2012, many of the families who had *restaveks* turned them out to fare for themselves on the streets. Having had their homes extensively damaged and their livelihoods severely curtailed, many of the families who had *restaveks* found these children to be burdens they didn't want to carry. During the days that followed the earthquake, thousands of discarded *restaveks* were wandering aimlessly on the streets of the city.

Such tragic stories of what happens to *restaveks* need not have happened if two things were true.

First, if this mother had had access to some means of employing birth control, the unwanted pregnancy would not have occurred and she might not have been lured into giving up her daughter. Christian relief agencies have tried to make family planning resources available to poor women in developing countries, but there are radio preachers here in America who condemn the distribution of condoms or birth control and the provision of the needed education for their use. They claim that making this available encourages elicit promiscuity, and they say that no Christian organization should be party to that. To say that such broadcasting can hurt the financial support base of these organizations is a great understatement. No child should be born into this world as unwanted or a burden.

Furthermore, the children who are born to any mother should be properly spaced. If children are born one after the other, without healthy spacing and timing of pregnancies, a mother can be faced with the necessity of nursing more than one child at a time. This can prove to be more of a strain than most good mothers could handle.

Second, child sponsorship can help mothers. Sponsoring a child through a Christian humanitarian organization such as World Vision or Compassion International could keep such mothers from being lured into giving away their children to become *restaveks*. Furthermore, in most cases, when a child is sponsored, the child's whole family benefits because it is likely that food would be shared. The daily cost for a sponsorship is less than half of what you would pay for a cup of coffee at Starbucks—so why not do it?

Of course, there also has to be an extensive education for men who, too often, refuse to use condoms and, even worse, take pride in siring as many children as possible to show off their sexual potency. Sadly, such men, after having refused to use condoms, regularly walk away from their pregnant partners, leaving behind impoverished mothers to do the best they can with the challenges that go with raising children.

When Christ initiated his ministry, he declared that he had come to declare "good news for the poor" (see Matthew 11:5; Luke 4:18). Considering those impoverished women in the back hills of Haiti, some of God's good news (in addition to hearing the good news about Jesus) is getting the means whereby they can control their biological destinies, not only for their own sakes, but also for the sake of their children.

Dr. Tony Campolo is a former professor emeritus at Eastern University, a founder of RedLetterChristians.org and the Campolo Center for Ministry, as well as a bestselling author and speaker.

Chapter 32

Speaking Up for Other Mothers

◄o► *Tracie Hamilton*

On January 12, 2010, I watched, as did the world, the horror and the shock at the extreme loss of life in Haiti. Mothers, fathers, and children died. Families were separated, never to reunite. People lost their lives in the rubble; people lost their limbs. The earthquake was almost an unfathomable crisis of biblical proportions.

As I sat watching my television in the comfort of my home, all I kept thinking was that I was desperate to get there to help and love these people. I could not look away. That could be me. That could be my own children. God truly burdened my heart with that natural disaster in Haiti. For some reason, it triggered this inside of me: No human life is more valuable than another. We are all equal in the eyes of God.

As a mother of two, how could I not empathize? How could I *not* do something? There was *and is* so much need, and so many people were dying. As I wrestled with the reality of this tragedy, I kept returning to the words of the prophet Jeremiah: " 'He defended the cause of the poor and needy. . . . Is that not what it means to know me?' declares the LORD" (22:16). My heart was there with them.

And so I prayed. I prayed for a year and a half. I prayed for the Haitian people, and I prayed for wisdom for what my husband, Scott, and I could do for them. A very dear and wise friend told us to wait in terms of our aid. Though we wanted to donate immediately, instinctively, he recommended that we simply wait to see who was and is still there after all the media and all the celebrities had left. Who would remain after the crisis fatigue had set in for everyone else? Who would be committed for the long haul?

Then we found a local group in Nashville, LiveBeyond. Dr. David Vanderpool and his wife, Laurie, were committed. They had been there in the midst of the earthquake with mobile medical care, including food and water and vaccines and primary care, but they were there to stay. Scott and I committed to travel with them to Haiti, and we went to the region of Thomazeau, just northeast of Port-au-Prince.

There was no water, electricity, or medical care. But these people survived and, at times, thrived. When we arrived, we rolled up our sleeves, and the Vanderpools put us to work in the health clinic. Even if we weren't health professionals, we were parents first and foremost. We could provide love, care, and prayer.

I have a clear memory of my first experience there, simply praying with a young mother and her baby. As I sat with this woman, I wondered how, if our lives had been switched, I might have felt in her place.

That same week, another mother, Gertrude, came in twice a day with her baby, who was near death. Thankfully, Dr. Vanderpool was able to successfully treat the little baby girl. Today Gertrude is a full-time employee with LiveBeyond and helps facilitate the maternal health program, and her little girl is thriving. Through this program, mothers and other women receive education for prenatal care, nutrition, and basic skills for childbirth. With the support of the maternal health staff, Gertrude counsels these young mothers on labor and delivery, breastfeeding, and caring for the infant, as well as postnatal care.

The staff's continuous support empowers these mothers to understand their self-worth and the value of their child's life. As a result of LiveBeyond's maternal health model, the perinatal mortality rate has substantially decreased by 66 percent in Thomazeau. Currently, there are more than 200 women enrolled in the program, with plans to double the enrollment within the next year.

Not every story like Gertrude's has ended with good news. Some children died. And we sat with parents and grandparents and grieved with them.

The drive of the Scriptures is to help the poor. There are more than 2,500 verses to remind us of that. We are called time and again to help the widow, the orphan, and the alien. James 1:27 calls this pure and faultless religion. Through our relationship with LiveBeyond, Scott and I have been able to live out this Scripture. We decided to take this literally. We will welcome two beautiful, bright children who have lost their parents into our home as our own.

The judgment parable Jesus shares in Matthew 25:37–39 reminds us all of what is truly important: providing the most basic of needs for the world's most vulnerable populations.

> "Then the righteous will answer him, 'Lord, when did we see you hungry and feed you, or thirsty and give you something to drink? When did we see you a stranger and invite you in, or needing clothes and clothe you? When did we see you sick or in prison and go to visit you?'"

There are more mothers like Gertrude who need food and drink and clothing, yes. But these mothers also need our support in helping them be healthier, happier mothers—to better plan their families and their futures for themselves and their children. We know how to do this. We just need to spread awareness and lend our voices so that we can get to this nexus of global health issues.

Join us in standing for the health of mothers and children worldwide, so that we may celebrate thriving children and families and life itself.

Tracie Hamilton is a philanthropist and mother of four children. She is married to Scott Hamilton, an Olympic gold-medalist, television personality, and philanthropist. They live in Franklin, Tennessee.

Chapter 33

Every Child Deserves a Family

◄○► Mary Beth Chapman

My involvement with issues surrounding maternal and child health began in 1997 when our oldest daughter, Emily, and I traveled to Haiti. It was my first time visiting a developing nation; I was heartbroken and challenged by what I saw and experienced. I will never forget walking the streets of Port-au-Prince, hand in hand with my daughter, and being approached by a Haitian mother with a young child on her hip. "Please, please, oh please!" she begged me. "Please, take my child with you!"

Her plea was one of loving desperation.

Reflecting on the sacrifice his son's birthmother made in choosing to place her child for adoption, theologian Miroslav Volf wrote, "She loved [my son] for his own sake, and therefore she would rather have suffered his absence if he flourished than to have enjoyed his presence if he languished."[1]

Often due to circumstances beyond a woman's control, mothers around the world feel forced to make a decision between her child's well-being and her familial integrity. I can't imagine the anguish and heartbreak these women experience, feeling incapable of fulfilling their desire to nurture and protect their own. Mothers and their children should be able to remain together. It is a bond and relationship that is not easily broken. A mother wants to provide the very best for her child, and she will go to great lengths to do so.

I think of the women who birthed our three youngest daughters; I can't imagine feeling coerced, whether it be because of extreme poverty,

---

1. Miroslav Volf, *Free of Charge* (Grand Rapids: Zondervan, 2005), 12.

oppressive sexism, or government regulations, to forever separate myself from my child.

Until that moment in 1997, paralyzing poverty and the subsequent issues rooted within were stories I heard about in the news. But on the streets of Port-au-Prince, I looked into the eyes of another mother, her narrative of anguish and helplessness abruptly interrupting mine. As a result of our trip to Haiti, a seed was planted in my heart that eventually grew into the nonprofit we now call Show Hope.

Co-founded by my husband, Steven, and me in 2003, Show Hope is a movement to care for orphans, restoring the hope of a family to orphans in distress around the world. Show Hope primarily does this by

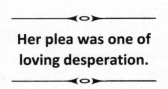

Her plea was one of loving desperation.

offering adoption aid financial grants that help give orphans forever families. Additionally, we provide care for particularly vulnerable orphans, those with physical and intellectual disabilities, through our Special Care Centers in China. Since its inception, Show Hope has helped provide forever homes through adoption aid grants for more than 4,500 orphans from more than fifty-two countries, including the United States. In addition, more than 1,600 orphans with disabilities have received critically needed medical care.

I, along with Steven and the staff at Show Hope, believe that every child deserves a family. Since Show Hope's first day of operations, we have been committed to a certain hierarchy of best practices in caring for orphaned and vulnerable children, wherein preservation of the birth family remains of paramount importance. Show Hope uses the PRAY acronym to remind ourselves that adoption should be appropriately considered within the following spectrum of care: Preservation of families, Reunification of families, Adoption, and Youth services such as foster care or community-based care. (Regarding adoption, we prefer in-country when possible and look to international adoption if a domestic placement is unlikely to occur.)

As we work toward restoring the hope of a family to orphans in distress, there are very real issues we must address. Every new life begins and is cultivated within, amidst, and among that of a mother's. Science and psychology reveal to us that the health and well-being of a mother is intimately linked to that of her baby. Steven and I are excited that Christians are joining their voices together to address these issues through the work of Hope Through Healing Hands' Faith-Based Coalition for Healthy Mothers and Children Worldwide.

We anticipate, with great hope, a world where mothers loving their children "for their child's own sake" looks like a family remaining together forever.

Mary Beth Chapman is The New York Times *bestselling author of* Choosing to SEE *and the president of Show Hope, an adoption awareness nonprofit organization she co-founded with her husband, Grammy Award-winning recording artist Steven Curtis Chapman. They live in Nashville, Tennessee, with their family.*

Part 4

Why Maternal
Health Matters to
People of Faith

‹O›

Dorine's Story
Burundi

In 1983, I was born the fifth child to a farmer mother and a soldier father in Muramvya, Burundi. In this small village we children ran free, playing handball with the other girls, running relay games, or playing hopscotch. I loved to play house as a child. We would make dolls and "cook" for our families with sticks and whatever else we could find.

I was expected to help with the chores around the house, and my responsibility was to fetch our family's water, since we had no running water at home. I'd walk to the well, fill our jug, and carry it home on my head. Many other young girls had the same chore, so I didn't feel alone doing this. I also helped look after our goats and do household chores such as cleaning and mopping the floors.

When I was six years old, I started primary school at Muramvya Primary School. It was an excellent school, built by Belgians and using their education system. It was a five-kilometer (3.1-mile) walk from home, which I walked every day.

When I was ten years old, my father, a soldier, was killed. My mother struggled, working very, very hard, to put me and my seven siblings through school. She had some help from my aunt, who took care of us and helped with school fees. I was able to graduate from Muramvya Secondary School and eventually went to Bujumbura to get my degree in nursing. At Mwaro University, a four-year school, I lived with other students in an apartment and shared tasks like cooking and shopping. I learned to be responsible and take care of myself, as well as learning more about what is required to be a proper nurse.

I hadn't always wanted to be a nurse. In fact, as a child my dream was to be a teacher. But my aunt, when I was young, explained to me the benefits of a more technical education, that I would make more money to support the family I hoped to have one day. I watched my uncle, a doctor, at work. When his patients were cured, they would come to his house, where I was living, and give gifts and thanks. We would share in those gifts and celebrations of healing.

I saw how thankful and happy people are when they are healed — that through medicine God could work through you to heal people. I wanted to do that, so I pursued nursing and eventually earned the highest level of nursing degree offered in Burundi, the A-0 qualification. My dream is still to pursue a Master's and PhD to get specialty qualifications, and I haven't given up on that entirely.

From the time I was a young child, I dreamed of getting married one day. I like babies and have always wanted to have a family. As a teenager, I had several boyfriends. But when I became a Christian, I decided to stop having all these boyfriends, because I understood that these physical relationships were not what Christ wanted for me, and I did not want to sin. I thought, instead, that I would focus on my studies and wait until after I graduated from the university to find a boyfriend, one I would want to marry.

> **Most Burundian Christians do not believe in family planning. The churches have told mothers it is a sin and if you do it, you won't go to heaven.**

When I was twenty-eight, I met a nice Christian man at my church. He was a leader in the Groupes Bibliques Universitaires (GBU), for which I became a leader when he left university. We kept in touch over that time, and eventually he proposed. I accepted right away, and we were engaged for two years before we married in a nice ceremony with many friends and family members. According to our local custom, my family held a dowry ceremony before the wedding at a church. I'm so happy to be married to this servant of God, one of the leaders in our church and a very good man.

Once we married, I got into the habit of tracking my monthly cycle, and two months into our marriage I recognized that I was late. My husband brought home a pregnancy test, which confirmed that I was expecting a baby. We were delighted, got down on our knees, and thanked God, but we were also scared. Through our prayers, we trusted that God would take care of all our needs related to this baby.

When the time came for him to be born, I went to the hospital and ended up having a caesarean section. We were thrilled to welcome our son to this world. It's a miracle, a true blessing, to have our son, Peniel. Doctors told me, however, that I should wait at least two years for my body to heal before we have another baby.

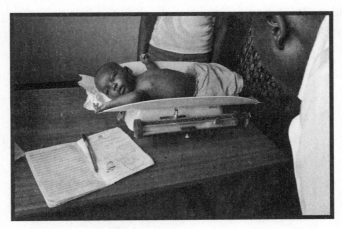

Some family members — my mother-in-law in particular — haven't liked our choice to use family planning. But my husband is supportive of my health and the health of my children. Being a mother in Burundi is not easy, because in our culture, mothers are solely responsible for their children. Mothers do their best to give their children what they need, but they don't have enough to give to them. You find a family with four to six children, and only the father might have a job. They may be in debt from loans. It's not easy. It's hard to describe how people live there, because if you compare the salary, it's not nearly the same as in the United States.

There is a proverb in Kirundi, my language, that says, *"Mundaharara inzara haka vyuka inzigu"* — which means that when you sleep with an empty stomach and its related troubles, you wake up in the morning with anger. This makes life hard for mothers in Burundi. When the father doesn't earn enough, they spend time outside working the field while their babies are hungry and crying. When a baby cries, it is so difficult for a mother.

On top of that, most Burundian Christians do not believe in family planning. The churches have told mothers it is a sin and if you do it, you won't go to heaven. There are many beliefs about family planning that are not true. We need more training for mothers so they can learn the truth. And with family planning, we can achieve better health for the mother and child, so mothers can contribute to their families by working if they desire to. We need this to help our families and our communities.

Chapter 34

The Good Samaritan in the Global Village

◄○► *Jim Wallis*

I remember when Mrs. King and I were first in Jerusalem. We rented a car and drove from Jerusalem down to Jericho. And as soon as we got on that road, I said to my wife, "I can see why Jesus used this as the setting for his parable." It's a winding, meandering road. It's really conducive for ambushing.... That's a dangerous road. In the days of Jesus it came to be known as the "Bloody Pass." And you know, it's possible that the priest and the Levite looked over that man on the ground and wondered if the robbers were still around. Or it's possible that they felt that the man on the ground was merely faking, and he was acting like he had been robbed and hurt, in order to seize them over there, lure them there for quick and easy seizure. And so the first question that the priest asked—the first question that the Levite asked was, "If I stop to help this man, what will happen to me?" But then the Good Samaritan came by. And he reversed the question: "If I do not stop to help this man, what will happen to him?"

—*Martin Luther King Jr.*[1]

Almost everybody knows the story of the Good Samaritan and how Jesus told it to answer a question somebody had asked him: "Who is my neighbor?" That is always a good question. But we need to ask it in the right context. Helping a man in need by the side of a dangerous road was the example Jesus used to show who our neighbor is and how to help him or her. Who is our neighbor? In our increasingly connected global world, this ancient moral question takes on a whole new context. What does it mean for the Good Samaritan to go global?

The very famous parable of the Good Samaritan is widely understood to be one of Jesus' key teachings on ethics. And it concerns a question that

---

1. Martin Luther King Jr., "I've Been to the Mountaintop" (speech, April 3, 1968, Mason Temple, as transcribed on "Top 100 American Speeches"), *American Rhetoric*, http://www.americanrhetoric.com/speeches/mlkivebeentothemountaintop.htm.

was fundamental in ancient times and remains so in the modern world: Who is my neighbor? With our world now becoming so globalized and closely connected, it is a question we will need new ethical perspectives and patterns to deal with. This story can help us.

Martin Luther King Jr. spoke about this parable and the plight of those robbed and beaten on the roadways of life and the self-protecting avoidance of those who pass by on the other side—even religious leaders. Just as Jesus did, King was calling for a radical extension of the idea of the neighbor, well beyond the boundaries that people use to justify their lack of response to human suffering.

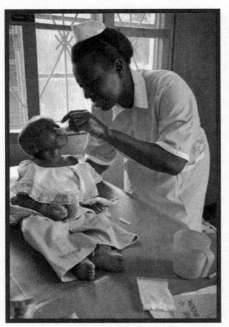

And that is what this parable is all about: expanding and extending the identity of "our neighbor." There is no doubt that most human beings believe they have obligations and responsibilities to their neighbors. But they also believe in boundaries, and many people fall outside of them to become *nonneighbors*. It's much easier when our neighbor is a relative or friend or member of our group and very much like *us*. But when we have to cross boundaries—like race, religion, neighborhood, region, culture, class, tribe, country, and often gender, even within those other boundaries—the justifications begin for our having ignored somebody or some group of people.

One of the details that is so remarkable about this story is that Jesus intentionally points out that he's been stripped naked and left for dead. There is no way to identify him in the usual ways—his dress, his speech or dialect. The boundaries have disappeared, and the priest, the Levite, and the Samaritan have to decide without these helpful hints whether or not they would be this man's "neighbor." But for any number of reasons—self-preservation, ritual purity, or the fact that they were just too busy—the priest and the Levite moved over to the other side of the road and kept on walking.

The Good Samaritan, however, crossed all kinds of boundaries and took all sorts of risks by helping somebody in need. And that is the point Jesus is making. Humanity wants to put up boundaries, but Jesus is telling us to cross cultural, racial, religious, regional, and tribal boundaries to find our neighbors. There are no "non-neighbors" in this world. All of God's children are our neighbors, and that radical concept is absolutely essential to the idea of the common good. Indeed, it is a spiritual foundation for the common good.

> **Jesus is telling us to cross cultural, racial, religious, regional, and tribal boundaries to find our neighbors. There are no "non-neighbors" in this world.**

This basic ethic from the Good Samaritan parable needs to be the moral guide and compass for us now in an increasingly globalized world. And the good news is that it is being adopted and enacted by many of the brightest and most committed members of the next generation. To think of their neighbors across the world as easily as right next door is coming naturally to younger people, who have a far more global perspective of life than their parents do.

One facet of suffering that many people in the church are seeking to relieve is the devastatingly high maternal mortality rates that plague most of the developing world. More than 287,000 women die each year giving birth, and 99 percent of those deaths occur in regions marked by extreme poverty. Eighty percent of these deaths are preventable through timely prenatal and postnatal care, skilled birth attendants during delivery, and the availability of emergency care to deal with complications. Complications from pregnancy should not be the number one reason teen girls die worldwide.[2] No mother should die because she delivers in unsanitary conditions or hemorrhages at birth, with no doctor or midwife present. And no child

---

2. World Health Organization, "Adolescent Pregnancy," *Fact Sheet*, no. 364 (September 2014), http://www.who.int/mediacentre/factsheets/fs364/en/.

bride should be forced to endure an unwanted sexual relationship with a man twice her age or to bear him multiple children before she reaches her sixteenth birthday.

The good news is that by raising our voices to support access to contraception for women who want it, to teach women about reproduction and the healthy timing and spacing of pregnancy, and to train and dispatch more and more midwives each year to work with women in the most rural and poorest parts of the world, we can relieve their suffering. We are, in essence, lifting the wounded man from the side of the road and taking him to the inn, not hesitating to help even though it will come at a cost to ourselves.

The ethics of "who my neighbor is" are changing—for the better. The moral compass for that change is derived from our most ancient religious traditions but is now being picked up by the youngest members of our globalized world. We are called to play the Good Samaritan on life's roadside, wherever we directly encounter people in need; but that will only be an initial act. One day we must come to see that in order to protect women and children from being beaten and robbed as they make their journey on life's highway, the Jericho road must be transformed! And that commitment is all about the common good.

Jim Wallis is the president and founder of Sojourners. This article is adapted from "The Good Samaritan Goes Global," in The (Un)Common Good *by Jim Wallis (Grand Rapids: Brazos Press, a division of Baker Publishing Group, 2014). Used by permission.*

Chapter 35

The First-Responder Church

◄○► *Santiago "Jimmy" Mellado*

Garbage dumps make horrible delivery rooms—but Cristina had no choice. As she went into labor, her mother's wood-and-tin shack in a Philippines garbage dump served as birthing center, delivery room, and nursery.

I wasn't prepared to see a newborn there. I had gone to the dump with a team from Compassion International to see how one of our partner churches in Cebu City ministers to families who live in extreme poverty. Cristina lay exhausted on a mat spread over a cane floor inches above the dirt. Her son, Jonel, was an hour-and-a-half old. He slept next to her, swaddled in a T-shirt. The heat was oppressive, the smell fetid. But Cristina's mom, a volunteer at Compassion's child development center in the Mandaue City Baptist Church, had helped her daughter deliver Jonel.

I considered the realities that Cristina and her son faced in a home in the middle of the garbage. Platitudes are anemic at a time like that. I knew God had placed our Compassion team right there at that precise moment. The time was opportune for the Church to be the Church.

When the church works right, her effectiveness is unsurpassed. Nowhere is that more evident than when the church is a first responder. Nowhere is the need for a first responder more urgent than for an expectant mother or mother with an infant in the grip of abject poverty. Abject poverty is the stupid, debilitating poverty that weakens bodies, stunts hope, and perpetuates itself across generations. While her infant may only weigh a few pounds, the load of an impoverished mother is heavy. She is the last to go to bed and the first to get up in the morning. Too often she is the last to eat, if she eats at all. Too often she is uneducated, because the opportunity was given to a male in the family. And too often her opinion doesn't count, even when it comes to family planning and the spacing of her children.

This is where the church can be her best, not because she can do something *for* the poor, but because she will walk closely *with* the poor. There is a world of difference between the two. In Compassion International's partnership with local churches in some of the world's most impoverished communities, "with" is the operative word. Hundreds of the 6,500-plus churches with which Compassion partners implement a Child Survival Program that walks side by side with mothers-to-be and new moms. From the womb through toddlerhood, the church assigns a child survival specialist to nurture a one-to-one, woman-to-woman relationship. The experience is life-changing.

For many of these moms, just the idea that they actually matter is transformative in its own right. Her physical health in pregnancy is monitored biweekly through home visits by her child survival specialist. The assurance of an attended birth takes away her isolation and eliminates the fear of delivering a child alone.

> **This is where the church can be her best, not because she can do something for the poor, but because she will walk closely with the poor. There is a world of difference between the two.**

And after delivery, the child survival specialist maintains a regular schedule of relationship and care. Everything from nutrition and health to toddler development and home safety is explored in biweekly visits. This is a church-based first responder approach inside the home and inside the life of a mother and her infant.

Walking *with* also brings mothers together. Each month, moms in the Child Survival Program gather at the local church, where the woman-to-woman relationship is magnified in a women-to-women community. In an environment of relationship and trust, the church contextualizes the concepts of family planning and birth spacing.

For many women this is their first hint that they can directly influence their own family's future. What should be obvious actually flies in the face of messages they receive in their neighborhoods. Older women in their families who could help the young mothers understand their options may inadvertently communicate an entrenched cultural view of frequent, unplanned pregnancies. Their own lack of understanding and the cultural momentum of tradition become unintended barriers.

The church's first responder approach counters negative patterns of family planning and mistrust that have permeated communities for generations. In the spiritual context of Jesus' teachings and inside a community of support, mothers receive a new message of freedom that expresses itself in all areas of life from personal grace to expressions of freedom and influence in life's most intimate decisions. Paul's declaration in 2 Corinthians 3:17, "Now the Lord is the Spirit, and where the Spirit of the Lord is, there is freedom," finds practical applications in the church. Freedom in Jesus to discover self-worth and relationship with him. Freedom to escape illiteracy. Freedom to learn a marketable skill. And freedom and instruction on the specifics of family planning. A mom learns how to have critical conversations with her husband, and in many cases, the child survival specialist will accompany and assist her.

When the church works right, the peripheral vision of a mother in poverty begins to widen to the personal benefits of literacy, solid child development, and healthy spacing and timing of pregnancy.

Back in the Philippines, our Compassion staff and the church pastor secured an immediate place for Cristina and Jonel in Compassion's Child Survival Program. Now the local church would rally around Cristina to help her develop income-generating skills. They would train and assist her in nutrition, health checkups, and the life-forming needs of an infant as Jonel grows. The church and its Child Survival volunteers would do everything in their power to keep Jonel from being one of almost 19,000 kids under five who die every day from causes that rarely affect our children in the United States. Cristina and Jonel would receive loving, Jesus-centered care. Compassion would be accessible for Cristina. But more important, the church would walk with her and her son through their journey ahead.

Nevertheless, in God's sovereignty, here was a newborn with a mother who lived and sweated and eked out an existence amid the garbage. I wondered what God had in mind for this little boy. You see, the easy conclusion for Jonel to make as he grows older is that he is worthless: "My mother sifts garbage. I was born in the dump. My life and my future are worth nothing more than the next truck that dumps another soggy load of garbage at my feet."

No child should think like that. I knew there was no other place I needed to be than right there, right then. So I prayed. Not a quick, expected "bless them" prayer, but a heartfelt, Spirit-led plea to Jonel's heavenly Father.

As our interpreter translated, I asked God that Jonel's life would have value. I thanked God that his mother had come to Christ and had been baptized a month earlier. I prayed that Jonel's parents would love him the way Jesus does and that he would come to know Jesus as early as possible. I prayed for God to intervene and help Jonel realize his full potential in Jesus. I don't fully remember all I asked God for, but I'll never forget the intensity of the Spirit interceding in that home that day. And I said good-bye with a different spirit.

Once again I realized how relentlessly the church tracks down poverty in the most rancid of spaces. Because the church is there, because the church is a first responder, I left confident that Cristina and Jonel were going to make it. This was the church at her best. This was the church working the way it should and building a future—even when the future was just an hour-and-a-half old.

––––––––––––––

Santiago "Jimmy" Mellado is the president and CEO of Compassion International, a leading authority in holistic child development through sponsorship. Jimmy married his wife, Leanne, in 1986 and they have three adult children.

Chapter 36

You Just Never Know

◄○► *Mike Glenn*

When telling the Christmas story, we always take a few minutes to boo the innkeeper. He deserves it. After all, what kind of man would make an obviously pregnant woman go to the barn to sleep and deliver her baby there? There's just one problem with this story. The innkeeper is never mentioned. We've made up the whole story.

What if the innkeeper and his wife, upon seeing Joseph and the very pregnant Mary, tried their best despite the circumstances? With the inn being crowded, the couple could have decided the barn was the best place for Mary. Maybe if the hay was stacked up just right and the blankets were laid around, Mary would have been given a warm, comfortable—and private—place to have her baby.

And Jesus was born. The Son of God was wrapped in swaddling clothes and placed in a manger. God was welcomed into our world, and the climactic stanza of God's redemption song was begun ... by a baby.

A baby that would need help to survive. He would have to be held, fed, bathed, and dressed. If Jesus was going to have any chance to make his mark on the world, Mary and Joseph would have to take very good care of him. I think you will agree with me: Mary and Joseph did pretty well.

As Christ followers, we believe every person bears the *imago dei*. That is, every person brings something of God's likeness to the world. Like any great art, the work reveals the Artist. Every person is a piece of the mosaic of creation that makes Christ

> ◄○►
> **Each piece, while not beautiful or significant in itself, congeals in beauty — in its place — with the countless other pieces to reveal an overwhelming and transforming image of God.**
> ◄○►

known. Each piece, while not beautiful or significant in itself, congeals in beauty—in its place—with the countless other pieces to reveal an overwhelming and transforming image of God.

The loss of one piece diminishes the *imago dei*. The loss of one person, the inability of one person to fulfill all he or she was created to be, leaves our experience with God incomplete and frustrated.

This is the reason Christ followers are committed to the issues of maternal and child health care. Clean water, good prenatal care, and proper nutrition are spiritual as well as physical issues. To diminish the person diminishes the possibilities of knowing Christ in all of his fullness.

So here we are. Like our made-up innkeeper in the Christmas story, we are opening the door to a woman and her unborn child and considering what we have to do. Maybe we can't fix everything. Maybe we can't save everyone. But like the innkeeper on that fateful night, let's choose to do what we can. A few blankets, a little milk, a safe place—these simple acts are the stuff of miracles.

This is why our concern must be changed into a determined action. We must decide not to let anyone or anything keep us from helping this one child. After all, like our innkeeper, we may be surprised by whom we welcome into the world.

Mike Glenn is the senior pastor at Brentwood Baptist Church in Nashville, Tennessee. He and his wife, Jeannie, have two married sons.

Chapter 37

Blessed for All Generations

◄○► *Dan Scott*

> The dragon stood in front of the woman who was about to give birth, so that it might devour her child the moment he was born.
>
> *—Revelation 12:4*

Whatever we make of the seemingly infinite interpretations of this mysterious portion of Scripture, we can hardly miss at least this one point: the writer of the Revelation has a very high regard for motherhood and is deeply concerned about the dangers that lurk to derail God's plan to renew the earth through this woman and child.

However we interpret this particular passage, it reveals a deeply held Christian sentiment. No Christian can fail to be moved by knowing a mother has to give birth in unsanitary conditions. It sounds too much like the story of the baby born in a stable "because there was no room in the inn." No Christian can bear the thought of infanticide, either intentional or as a by-product of war. It sounds too much like the wail of "Rachel for her children because they are gone." Reports of such conditions will move Christian hearts because they are echoes of our own sacred story.

When Christians realize that women and children suffer, they will usually try to do something about it. The question, though, is whether we can learn to see the subtle ways in which that suffering continues. If we cannot see it, then despite our sentiments about the ancient suffering of our spiritual heroes, we can become more like the indifferent innkeeper, or even like Herod, both being determined not to acknowledge the difficult realities around them.

Christians confess to belief in "the Holy Spirit, the Lord, the Giver of Life." We should also learn to acknowledge how women and children are special instruments through which God's life comes. The cruel fact is that it is the very promise of life that so often robs women of their own lives.

The female body, for example, tangibly manifests the possibilities for nurture, ecstasy, and companionship that men intently desire. Thus, the female body can be marketed and purchased in overt and covert ways, including evils such as trafficking and pornography. The children, meanwhile, may be seen as either expendable inconveniences to that exploitation or products that may be groomed for future racketeering.

Nor are these blatant ills the only, or even the major, expressions of ways in which women and children suffer. In most cases, it is ignorance, that ancient and unintentional foe, that robs the world's women and children of health, personhood, and life. When a child barely into puberty gives birth to another, she often loses the possibility of living any sort of real life of her own. When soon thereafter she gives birth to another and then to yet another; when her companion, who in most cases would not intentionally cause her harm, must fight in a war he did not begin and has no power to stop; when he dies or returns home unable to work or full of a rage he cannot control; when he has no understanding of disease and carries to his wife an illness he contracts from another; when there is not enough food, enough education, enough medical help, enough knowledge — the center of the system of woe that results from this misery is a woman aged far beyond her years, struggling to stay alive another day and escape the wrath of the dragon.

> **Ignorance, that ancient and unintentional foe, robs the world's women and children of health, personhood, and life.**

Surely this is a possible reading of St. John's Apocalypse, for even if such a scenario does not describe the end of time of the world, it certainly describes the end of someone's world. Such scenes must stir the compassionate hearts of any human being anywhere, but especially the hearts of Christians, who confess their love and devotion for a man who died so that others could live.

How, then, do we address the suffering of the world's women and children? The New Testament tells us that it is only through love. Furthermore, that love cannot be mere sentiment. As the apostle James puts it, "Suppose a brother or sister is without clothes and daily food. If one of you says to them, 'Go in peace; keep warm and well fed,' but does nothing about their physical needs, what good is it?" (2:15–16). We are rather to treat a suffering mother as we would the mother of our Lord. We are to treat a child as though that child were the Savior of humankind.

At Christmastime we sing about "Good King Wenceslas," who on the Feast of Saint Stephen looked out of his palace window to see a poor man hunting firewood. We call this king "good" because he left the palace to find food and clothing for the shivering man in the cold. The rarely sung last verse says,

> In his master's steps he trod,
> where the snow lay dented.
> Heat was in the very sod
> which the saint had printed.
> Therefore, Christian men, be sure,
> wealth or rank possessing,
> Ye who now will bless the poor
> shall yourselves find blessing.

We address the needs of women and children in this spirit, by the incarnational move from our own comfort to join the discomfort of others. We help those, of whatever faith and spiritual walk, who are already engaged in the work of healing. We do not impose, we do not coerce, we do not control; we serve, for the sake of the One for whom the woman flees into the wilderness to escape the dragon's fiery breath.

Dan Scott is the senior pastor at Christ Church in Nashville, Tennessee, as well as a published songwriter, musician, and author. He is a husband, father to two daughters, and grandfather to four granddaughters.

Chapter 38

What Kind of People Ought You to Be?

◄○► *Jennie Allen*

But the day of the Lord will come like a thief. The heavens will disappear with a roar; the elements will be destroyed by fire, and the earth and everything done in it will be laid bare.

Since everything will be destroyed in this way, what kind of people ought you to be? You ought to live holy and godly lives as you look forward to the day of God and speed its coming. That day will bring about the destruction of the heavens by fire, and the elements will melt in the heat. But in keeping with his promise, we are looking forward to a new heaven and a new earth, where righteousness dwells.

—2 Peter 3:10–13

The apostle Peter talks about the end of time. We won't see it coming. But then there's this incredible statement tucked in there: "Since everything will be destroyed ... what kind of people ought you to be?"

This is stunning, isn't it? If we believe that God is real and heaven will be our home one day, then this matters. If we hope for it to come, if we look forward to the day of God and "speed its coming," because we know we're going to live there in all this glory forever, then we have to ask ourselves, *What sort of people ought we to be?* Now, here.

How am I going to live out what I believe on this earth?

Let's look at this question in light of the oppression of women that exists all over the face of this earth now. *Right now.* Oppression is born of an assumption that women—and usually their children, too—are in some way inferior or have less value than the men around them.

This doesn't begin as formal government action. No governor or dictator says, out of nowhere, that the women in his village or country can't vote or be educated. This oppression begins in our souls. Fears shape our thoughts. Thoughts become culture, and culture defines laws. So when we look out into the world and see oppression of women, we have to remember that it began in the souls of humans. With a belief. With a fear.

The result is the greatest social problem of the twenty-first century. Hillary Clinton said it "remains the great unfinished business of the twenty-first century."[1] Because it affects everything. It affects the way children are raised. It affects education. It affects poverty. It affects the fact that AIDS is being spread all over the world. It affects health and wellness and quality of life.

It affects everything.

The numbers are staggering: 1 million children forced into prostitution every year, 3 million women sold as sex slaves, and more women are likely to be maimed or killed by male violence than by cancer, malaria, traffic accidents, and war combined. More girls have been killed in the last decade just for being girls than all the men in all of the wars of the last century.[2]

You can't tell me we don't have a problem here. We have a problem that is starting in our souls. And we have to start with our souls before we go try to fix another country's souls.

Let's be honest, though: The debate about the role of women speaking and leading in the church is one of the most difficult, intense topics that we have in our Christian communities. I want you to know that I'm coming from a conservative place on this topic. But I happen to have a husband who is secure in himself, and he's not afraid of my strengths and gifts, which have given me a platform, as a woman, to be part of speaking up and solving the problem. Yet, some days I don't exactly know how to solve this problem, because I have four people who need to eat three meals a day and somehow get to basketball practice too. But at the end of my life, I'm going to have to stand before God, and I'm going to have to answer for more than just my people in my house.

---

1. Jaime Fuller, "Hillary Clinton Says Equality for Women Is the 'Great Unfinished Business of the 21st Century,'" *The Washington Post*, March 7, 2014, http://www.washingtonpost.com/blogs/post-politics/wp/2014/03/07/hillary-clinton-says-equality-for-women-is-the-great-unfinished-business-of-the-21st-century/.

2. Nicholas D. Kristof and Sheryl WuDunn, *Half the Sky* (New York: Random House, 2009).

I'm going to have to answer for every good work that God prepared in advance for me to do. Are we doing the good works that God prepared in advance for us to do? When you look around this broken, weary world and see the oppression of women—the ones who don't have freedom with their husbands or in their communities to make even the most basic decisions about their health—can we see the fruit of the good works God has prepared for us to do?

I don't want that to make you feel guilty, because in many places in this world, the answer is yes. Women and men of faith are spreading a life-giving sense of community and support, but there are still so many places where support is needed. Because healthy relationships move us to wholeness and action. I believe there are several answers to the problem of oppression of women, but the one I am going to give my life to—in the name of Jesus Christ—is friendship.

I have a good friend named FeeFee in Haiti. She pops popcorn every day for her kids. I pop popcorn for my kids when they come from school. She pops popcorn and sells it bag by bag for her kids to be able to go to school. FeeFee's kids don't need sponsorship. She's taking care of them. What FeeFee needs is not for us to come in and rescue her with our money.

We mistake people for projects. We mistake need for weakness. We mistake struggle for pity. If you teach a woman to fish or sew or pop popcorn and turn her loose, watch the pride that wells, the stories that are built, the children who are unleashed, the countries that are restored. She needs men and women in the body of Christ to help lift her head and remind her, on those really discouraging days, that she is taking care of her own people. Because that woman is proud that she takes care of her own people. We need to be thinking of ways to come alongside women's passion to care for their families.

Women and men of faith, let's take care of the mommas. Because we will take care of all the babies when we do. The fight against the oppression of women is in the lifting of heads. I want to be a head lifter. I think that's why God put me on earth, and I think that's why God put you on earth too—to lift heads to see that there's a God who loves you and esteems you and does not see you as inferior.

Here are three steps that the church can take to help in releasing women and lifting heads:

1. Men, we need you in this fight. We need you to protect women and fight for them. Jesus fought for them. He saw them hurting, and he ran to them, over and over. He lifted their heads and blessed them, met their needs, and took care of them.

2. We can't be so hard on each other. Some are called to go to the ends of the earth; some are called to stay at home. Obedience is the most important thing. Let's support each other in our different callings to meet needs in this world.

3. Women, make sure you are not holding back because you feel as if you can't help. We are equipped more than any other generation in the world to make a significant impact for Christ. Almost every day I see need, and we can meet some of it. If you know my Jesus, you were rescued. You were fought for. You were bought. You were saved. And you are filled with the Holy Spirit of God.

He has plans and purposes that he chose in advance for you to walk in. Some of those plans are babies at home in diapers and soup in Crock-Pots, but some of them are people like FeeFee who are popping popcorn and could use a friend.

We have the opportunity to meet needs, but it will start in small ways. It will start by believing in other women. It will start by building relationships and not throwing solutions at problems. It will start by being brave enough to obey God — whatever it is he is calling you to do.

Let's let our generation's legacy be that we loved really well — that we loved this world really well. And we actually got to be a part of releasing and engaging and empowering women to change their own communities.

Jennie Allen is an author, speaker, and the founder and visionary of IF:Gathering. She lives in Austin, Texas, with her family.

Chapter 39

On Shame and Stewardship: A Pastor's Perspective

◄○► *Scott Sauls*

The longer I am a pastor, the more convinced I become that every person, regardless of her or his situation, is fighting a hidden battle with shame. Shame, the greatest enemy of God's grace and also the greatest inhibitor of truth, justice, and human love, is something that must be addressed if a dysfunctional human community is to become functional, healthy, and mutually supportive.

Shame — the terrifying sense that something is deeply wrong with us — keeps us preoccupied with ourselves and inattentive to the needs of others. Shame tells us falsely that we need to fix ourselves before we can focus on serving others. It tells us we must get our act together before we can act on behalf of the poor, the lonely, the oppressed, and the marginalized. Before we can give attention and energy to paving paths of flourishing in the developing world, we must first develop our own sense of purpose and our own sense of self. *Charity starts at home*, we tell ourselves. If we don't take care of ourselves first, then we won't be able to care effectively for others. If we don't get healthy ourselves, we will be limited in our ability to invest in important causes like maternal health in the developing world.

In a way, we assume correctly. When Adam and Eve's shame was exposed in the garden, they both turned immediately inward. Adam shifted his attention away from God and Eve and toward the search for fig leaves to cover himself and to hide his shame. Eve did the same. Man and woman sought independence from God, lost interest in one another's flourishing, and looked out for number one. Adam blamed Eve for their new predicament. Then Adam blamed God. Eve blamed the serpent.

Adam and Eve set the tone for the rest of us. Ever since Eden, every man, woman, and child has been facing a hidden battle with shame. The vague sense that there is something deeply wrong with us compels us to hide, blame, and run for cover. Left to ourselves, we are restlessly turned inward and desperately committed to some kind of self-salvation strategy. We work hard to create a counter-narrative to the shaming voice within and without. It's just that our fig leaves in the developed world have become more sophisticated than the ones Adam and Eve used to cover themselves. Our fig leaves are represented in the ways that we compensate for the failed expectations that others place on us and that we place on ourselves.

Before relocating to Nashville in 2012 to assume the role of senior pastor of Christ Presbyterian Church, I was ministering in an area of New York City with a high concentration of men and women who worked in finance. When the Great Recession hit in 2008, and as financial institutions crashed and careers were ruined, many people expressed a feeling that they had lost not only money and a career, but also a sense of self. "When you work on Wall Street," they would say, "eventually you begin to believe that you *are* what you do, and you *are* what you make."

The question "What is she worth?" is taken quite literally. The metrics of human value are measured in terms of salaries and bonuses. When the salary and the bonus disappear or get cut, so does the worth of the person. This becomes true, not only in his peers' eyes, but also in his own eyes. One multibillionaire lost half of his net worth in the crash. Though he was still a multibillionaire, and though nothing about his quality of life had changed, he committed suicide. The shame of losing rank in the pecking order of the financial world turned him completely inward and caused him to self-destruct.

Shame is also a significant issue in the developing world. The only difference is the form of currency that determines a person's worth. Whereas we may determine someone's worth based on the size of her or his financial portfolio, women in Uganda are assigned value by society and especially by the men in their lives on the basis of their ability to produce children.

Ugandan women are expected from a very young age—as early as thirteen and even younger—to produce scores of children. If a woman can survive these pregnancies and childbirth complications and her children live, she is seen as valuable currency. If a woman is infertile, she is seen as cursed. This creates an environment in which women are under constant pressure to perform and produce, both sexually and maternally, because a failure to do so would bring shame upon them by society and by the men in their lives.

What if there were a way for the cycle of shame to be broken in our lives? What if there were a way to divorce ourselves from the pressures that culture puts on us to be rich or beautiful or well-respected or, in the case of Ugandan women, to be only producers of children? What if there were a way for the pressure to be relieved, in both the developed and developing world, to perform and achieve and measure up in order to be a person of value? What if we no longer felt a need to prove ourselves, to validate our own existence in the world's eyes and also in our own eyes? What if our secret battle with shame were neutered, freeing us to turn our attention away from ourselves and toward neighbors who are near to us, and also toward neighbors—such as Ugandan women—who are on the other side of the world and need our partnership and support? What if there were a way that we, having had our shame undone, could also contribute to the undoing of shame experienced by these women?

> **What if our secret battle with shame were neutered, freeing us to turn our attention away from ourselves and toward our neighbors?**

My greatest joy as a Christian pastor is that I get to tell people that such a remedy exists. When Jesus allowed himself to be stripped naked, spit upon, taunted, rejected, and made nothing on the cross—when he, the one who had nothing to be ashamed of, surrendered to the ruthless, relentless shaming that led to our redemption and healing—he accomplished our liberation from shame. He who was rich became poor for our sakes, that through his poverty we might become rich.

But our riches are more solid, so much more solid, than mere material riches. Our riches are the kind that free us from having to be affluent or thin or intelligent or networked or famous or sexually attractive or fertile or anything else that the world says we must be in order to have value. Our riches are the kind that assure and reassure us that we have nothing left to hide, nothing left to fear, and nothing left to prove.

Because Jesus took on himself the full freight of our shame, we no longer have to exhaust ourselves with endless and futile efforts to make something *of* ourselves. We now have an inner resource that can liberate us from preoccupation with self. We now have an inner resource that frees us to treat all people as our equals. We now have an inner resource that endearingly and compellingly invites us to join God in his mission to love.

At an awareness dinner in Nashville, Melinda Gates told a room full of pastors, leaders, culture makers, and influencers why she and her husband, Bill, decided to devote their lives and resources to helping people in the developing world. Her reason is plain and simple and traces back to what she was taught as a child through her Catholic upbringing: *Every person is equal.* "There is no reason," Mrs. Gates said, "why a woman in the developing world shouldn't have health care and education and running water and opportunity just like I do. Because a woman in the developing world is equal to me."

The notion that every person is equal is one to which any reasonable person will give mental assent. But when we come to understand that Jesus has taken our shame from us, and that because of this we have nothing left to hide, nothing left to fear, and nothing left to prove, we become *owners* of, and not mere assenters to, the notion that every person is equal. Our energies shift from being preoccupied with self to being preoccupied with God and the flourishing of our neighbor.

Dr. Martin Luther King Jr. took this affirmation further, reminding us not only *that* every person is equal, but *why* every person is equal:

> The whole concept of the image of God is the idea that all men have something within them that God injected.... And this gives him a uniqueness, it gives him worth, it gives him dignity. And we must never forget this...: there are no gradations in the image of God. Every man from a treble white to a bass black is significant on God's keyboard, precisely because every man is made in the image of God. One day we will learn that. We will know one day that God made us to live together as brothers and to respect the dignity and worth of every man.[1]

Because of the way that Jesus valued you on the cross, and because you are the image of God, you are among the holiest objects that will ever be presented to God, to your fellow human beings, and even to yourself in the mirror. Is this enough, and will this *be* enough, to relieve you of your own hidden battle with shame? Will it be enough to free you from a love-hindering, tiring preoccupation with self?

Because your neighbors who are near, as well as your neighbors on the other side of the world who need you, are also the image of God and are your equals, you have a privilege and responsibility to participate, as God leads you, in his mission to advance his kingdom in truth, beauty, love, and justice on earth ... and to every square inch of the earth ... as it is in heaven. Is this enough, and will this *be* enough, to stimulate your imagination as to how you can steward and share your privilege?

May it be so.

Scott Sauls is the senior pastor of Christ Presbyterian Church in Nashville, Tennessee, and the author of Jesus Outside the Lines: A Way Forward for Those Who Are Tired of Taking Sides. *He and his wife, Patti, have two daughters.*

---

1. Martin Luther King Jr., "The American Dream," a sermon at Ebenezer Baptist Church, Atlanta, Georgia (4 July 1965).

Chapter 40

Sovereign Over Us

◄○► *Michael W. Smith*

In April 1997, Debbie and I visited a children's hospital in Soweto, South Africa, with Franklin Graham and his Samaritan's Purse organization. As we walked through the halls of that hospital, visiting children with terminal illnesses who we knew would never be healed this side of heaven, our hearts broke. We knew that this pain and suffering was not God's desire for his children, but that his plan is for us to help, to be the ones who bring his love into these devastating circumstances.

> There is strength within the sorrow
> There is beauty in our tears
> And You meet us in our mourning
> With a love that casts out fear

These words are from my song "Sovereign Over Us,"[1] and they remind me of those days in the hospital in Africa. Because even in those dark and sad places of suffering here on earth, God meets us there. He wipes away our tears. But he wants more for his children than to live in this sadness.

God's heart for the poor and suffering is evident all throughout Scripture. In fact, it is the most often mentioned theme in the Bible: care for the poor. More than 2,500 verses are dedicated to this topic. The instruction we see in the parable of the bags of gold in Matthew 25:14–30 has been particularly meaningful to me as I work out the ways God has asked me to be involved.

In this story, the manager of the estate comes to his workers and gives them each some seed money to go and multiply to benefit the estate. Each worker goes off and produces different results, and the manager is satisfied with all of those who have come back with more riches for the community.

---

1. Written by Aaron Keyes, Jack Mooring, and Bryan Brown, © 2011 Thankyou Music.

In fact, the only one he chastises is the man who is too fearful to act, who hoards the money and refuses to take a risk.

God has given each one of us talents, just as the estate manager gave his workers this seed money. And it can be scary to step out and use those gifts—the skillfulness of a carpenter, the artistry of a dancer, the attention to detail of an accountant, or the loving hand of a mother. We fear rejection and failure, but we must use these gifts and share them with others in order to fulfill Jesus' prayer that life on earth would be as it is in heaven, to see God's kingdom come here to earth.

Debbie and I have recently been heartbroken about the health crisis so many mothers around the world face. Lack of good medical care during pregnancy and childbirth, as well as too many unintended pregnancies in too short a time period, have claimed the lives of too many mothers. I think of the children left behind, motherless, whose chances of survival to the age of five drop significantly with no mother in their lives.

What talents has God given you that you may help these mothers and children? Are you passionate about traveling to these regions to help administer the lifesaving supplies they need? Could you speak up from home—through your blog, by writing a song, by telling your friends? God's gifted you in a unique way, and you can glorify him by responding to his perfect love that has not forgotten us, by helping those who are poor and suffering, both at home and halfway around the world.

Michael W. Smith is a three-time Grammy Award winner who has sold more than 13 million albums in his music career. He and his wife, Debbie, live in Nashville, Tennessee.

Chapter 41

The Old New Thing

Still Walking with Jesus
Toward the Least of These

◄○► *Sarah Masen and David Dark*

"In a word, what I'm saying is, *Grow up*. You're kingdom subjects. Now live like it. Live out your God-created identity. Live generously and graciously toward others, the way God lives toward you."

—*Matthew 5:48, MSG*

In 2011 the extraordinary poet and dancer Maya Angelou came to Nashville. Thousands came to hear what she had to say. She could do that, you know!

She carried with her a decades-long earning of the American public's ears. In everything she was up to, she lived into a radical articulation of hope for people denied a place at the table of human kindness, and, everywhere she went, she set a new one with large-hearted welcome. We trusted her the way we often find we can't help but trust the people who create spaces where we're allowed, in a deep sense, to grow into our best selves. She became an expert thriver who blossomed in spite of the hostile and often murderous climate she grew up in. She was someone who languaged and danced her way through suffering into a more equitable future.

When I think of her, I think of Jesus. Both Maya and Jesus were born and raised under a crushing hierarchy of one people group being constantly dominated by another, and they both proclaimed, by word and deed, better ways of doing things. Both dreamed up and embodied an artfully practiced subversive resistance even as the backs of their people were against the wall. They each sought ways of spreading the table wider unto the outcast, the estranged, and even the enemy.

With all this in mind, I was particularly taken with a story Maya told of people approaching her and letting her know that they, like her, are Christian. She noted that she likes to reply with playful astonishment, "*What?!* Already? I've been trying *so hard* for *so long.*"

Though we get it wrong before getting it right so much of the time, I think it's true to say that we live for moments when our perceived ideas about what it means to have a go at being Christian are radically challenged. We so live for these moments that we're often loathe to attach the label to ourselves, lest we think of conversion to something as wide and wonderful as lived Christianity as a "done deal" or a "mission accomplished." Why not think of conversion to the outrageously hospitable love of God as an unendingly revolutionary process to which we submit ourselves anew every moment of every day? This calls for renewed attentiveness to the minute particulars of our sweet old world we like to say God *so* loves.

For starters, this means being present enough to the stories of those who suffer for lack of love (and by "love" we mean all that makes for human thriving: enough food and clean water, shelter, good health care, education, safe and beautiful neighborhoods) to recognize Wisdom when she comes knocking on our door. We look up a lot. We ask ourselves, "What are we missing? Who are we marginalizing when we say what we say? Are we using language of exclusion or embrace?"

> **Be present enough to the stories of those who suffer for lack of love to recognize Wisdom when she comes knocking on our door.**

We remember Jesus' script-flipping phrase, "You have heard it said, ... but I say to you ...," and have appropriated its spirit of reform for our own time to wonder more imaginatively how what was a concern to our people-loving Jesus in first-century Palestine might translate as walking justly, loving mercy, and living humbly in our own radioactive days. *Hear* the good news of God's word. He calls us to become larger in love and in solidarity with the vulnerable, to participate in our most imaginative relief work.

This is a unique time when good, global research in maternal, newborn, and child health can present radical documents of reality that help us see the facts on the ground and deepen our response to the new "least of these" in our midst. It is *still* the case that women and children are vulnerable to old inequalities that deny them physical security and access to healthy living. Do we hear, as Jesus did, the cry of the Syrophoenician woman who challenged him to see that even the dogs get the crumbs that fall from the master's table?[1] Do we hear the 220 million women's voices around the world ask how they can better plan their families so that their own children will not only survive, but thrive? Are we teachable the way Jesus was in that moment of profound script-flipping? And, not only do we hear these voices, but are we "living graciously and generously," taking action, and lending our own voices on behalf of these women and children?

May we begin to be attentive to and inspired by all the new avenues we're discovering for spreading the table of thriving we believe God has spread for us. It's a process we are always learning and converting to anew. Our Sister Maya goes before us.

David Dark is a professor of religion at Belmont University and the author of books on completive religion, including The Sacredness of Questioning Everything. *His wife, Sarah Masen, is a recording artist and potter. They live in Nashville, Tennessee, with their children.*

---

1. See Matthew 15:21–28; Mark 7:25–30.

Chapter 42

The Village Nearby

◄○► *Deborah Dortzbach*

I thought I would deliver my firstborn child by myself in a makeshift lean-to on a windswept hill far from a health facility. I was terrified.

There was no one to give me prenatal care. No one to coach me. No one to talk to about my fears. No emergency backup for complications. No one except ... soldiers, hovering.

I am a nurse and was taken hostage while pregnant by the Eritrean Liberation Front and held in a remote, desolate location near the Sudan border. One day, as I wandered in allowable short distances, I discovered others like myself in a nearby village. They were Tigre women, clustered around each other as they framed their nomadic huts. Some were pregnant; some had children tugging at their long, faded skirts as they stretched straw mats over simple poles. One woman stood alone. She had no children and looked sad and abandoned.

I went to these women, and we chatted, each in our own mother tongue, as together we thrust grass mats over the acacia sticks, bounced babies in our arms, and laughed at each other's strange expressions. I put their weathered hands on my bulging bump of baby, and they seemed to curiously question, "What are you doing here?"

I have had many years now to reflect on that question. I was eventually released, received good medical care, and delivered a healthy baby boy. But my newfound friends were never freed from the captivity of unsafe motherhood and the future opportunity to participate in decisions about their families and their own well-being. Were I to return to the same hill today, I wonder if they would ask me the very same question, in the past tense, and what my answer would be. "What *have* you done, for us?"

The Tigre moms and millions like them let us know that before us is a choice—to improve maternal health or to actually increase maternal harm through just doing nothing. While we get genuinely interested for a brief season or for some project silos in maternal health, we all know that the deeper issues of behavior and structural change take time and perseverance. Our commitments must be unswerving and unending.

Fundamentally, as Christians we work and strive to improve maternal health because it is about *valuing* who a woman is as God made her and treasures her, not because of a role or function, marital status, maternal status, or even because of need, as great as that may be. *Needs and resources will come and go — but the intrinsic worth of woman as God sees her will always warrant our highest efforts to esteem her and fight for her equality and full expression of honor, dignity, safety, and health.*

The account in the Gospels[1] of the bleeding woman healed by Jesus demonstrates this. The unnamed woman, bleeding for twelve years, was stigmatized, spiritually ostracized, extremely weak, and economically impoverished. Yet, drawn by the working of Christ in her life, she ventured into crowded social space and touched Jesus. He cared so deeply and so thoroughly for her that he allowed her blood-impure status to spiritually defile him. It instantly healed the woman.

What a beautiful picture for us of the spiritual healing soon to come through the defilement Jesus took upon himself on the cross! God chose the body of woman through which to be born (Mary) and now the body of a woman to bring a foreshadowing of his healing power through death. Can there be any doubt he loves, treasures, honors, and redeems women and seeks to bring his redemption and completeness to all humankind in brokenness and suffering?

It was not only during the time of Galilee that God was at work in women. God works powerfully today through his Spirit, his people, and his church. For instance, I found women gathered regularly in a small church in Mukuru, a poor urban community in Nairobi, Kenya. They supported each other with small savings and self-help groups, Bible studies, and lessons on family planning and health. They taught their daughters about rites of passage and becoming a woman God's way through abstinence before marriage. They learned about HIV/AIDS. When sick,

---

1. Matthew 9:20–22; Mark 5:25–34; Luke 8:43–48.

they served one another and community members, and when they found an abandoned baby in a latrine, one member took him home and adopted him.

Women in Burundi in 2012 to 2013 committed to improving the health of their entire families by spacing the frequency of their children, committing to exclusive breastfeeding, and learning about family planning, using methods they found appropriate for their beliefs. As a result, they discovered the joy of learning and supporting one another through 209 Care Groups[2] and 130 church and community groups. Family planning uptake increased significantly from a baseline of 16 percent to 50 percent (47.6 percent being reported as modern method use).

At the core of life in India is the family. However, many women have little say in negotiating family choices that affect them as well as having safe sex for themselves and security for their children. Trafficking of children and young girls into the sex trade as an alternative to crippling rural poverty is a threat in some areas.

> **In India, many women have little say in negotiating family choices that affect them as well as having safe sex for themselves and security for their children.**

A program known as Families for Life explores the significance and meaning of marriage through a Tamil proverb: "When sugar cane is bound tightly, what can the ants do?" The program is designed to cling to traditions and biblical truth that bind couples together in their marriage and identify and address the "ants" that may destroy relationships, health, and life itself. Developed with a strong woman's voice, the curriculum and program strengthen the value and equality of women in marriage, address communication, and seek to help husbands and wives develop friendship

2. Originally created by World Relief Mozambique in 1995, the Care Group Model is a global model that improves health outcomes through cascade training of community volunteers who educate and empower families to make wise decisions for good health, disease prevention, and care seeking. Thousands of volunteers, one for every ten households, meet biweekly in small groups called Care Groups for training and supervision. They then visit each of their assigned neighbors' homes to pass on the health information, achieving universal coverage that is equitable and sustainable.

and common bonds, mutual honor and respect, and commitments for life in marriage.

Mary's response to discovering her vulnerable maternal state and to being comforted by the assurance of God's working in her life was to "Magnify the Lord" (Luke 1:46) and to rest assured he would "Fill the hungry with good things" (Luke 1:53).

Today, what is your response to God at work in the world and in your life? What village is near you, and just what are you doing there?

Deborah Dortzbach is the director of Health and Social Development for World Relief. She and her husband lived in Africa for twenty-five years; now they live in Baltimore, Maryland. She is the mother of three and the grandmother of nine.

Appendix

What You Can Do

1. How You Can Become an Advocate

Our hope is that after reading the essays in *The Mother and Child Project*, you've become inspired to raise your voice for health and hope for the 220 million women worldwide who want to better time and space their children.

If you're wondering, *What can I do to help?*, you can make a difference with advocacy. Proverbs 31:8–9 calls us to "Speak up for those who cannot speak for themselves, for the rights of all who are destitute. Speak up and judge fairly; defend the rights of the poor and needy." We ask you to join us in speaking out for women and children around the world by promoting awareness in your community and advocating for them with your leaders.

Awareness: Share the Stories

We encourage you simply to share the stories from this book with your friends and family, church, schools, and community. Begin a conversation that will save lives. Facebook, Twitter, Google+, Instagram, and other social media outlets are excellent forums to start conversations and share powerful images related to maternal health in the developing world. If you have a website or blog, please write about what has inspired you in this book.

Follow us at @HTHHglobal on Twitter, HopeThroughHealingHands .com, or facebook.com/hopethroughhealinghands. We welcome you to share our statistics, posts, and web resources with your networks. Join us in speaking out for those who cannot speak, to defend the rights of the poor and needy.

Advocacy: Call or Write Your Leaders

Advocacy may be the most powerful gift you can offer. Consider calling your senator, representative, or the White House to let them know that you care deeply about maternal, newborn, and child health. Below is a sample letter you could write or email or use as a script for a phone call to let your leaders know you stand behind US leadership on the issues of maternal and child health and international family planning.

Date _____

Dear President/Senator/Representative _____ ,

As a constituent, I write to you to urge you to protect funding for US foreign assistance programs for both Maternal, Newborn, and Child Health and Family Planning.

As a person of faith, I care deeply about the health of mothers and children worldwide. Every year more than 287,000 women die, most of them in the developing world, from complications in pregnancy or childbirth. The good news is that we have the knowledge and tools to allow women to decide how best to time and space their pregnancies in a healthy way. However, more than 222 million women worldwide lack access to the effective contraceptives, counseling, or services they need for this. If this need were met, families would be empowered to make decisions about healthy timing and spacing of their pregnancies, saving the lives of both women and children.

We thus ask you to protect funding for US foreign assistance programs for both Maternal, Newborn, and Child Health and Family Planning.

Thank you for your service. We are counting on your leadership and support for mothers and children around the world.

Sincerely,

_____ name

_____ occupation

_____ address

_____ email

2. How You Can Give: Partners in Maternal and Child Health

Hope Through Healing Hands stands alongside a number of excellent organizations that provide services for women and children around the world. We encourage you to learn more about the organizations below, some mentioned within the essays, and how you can support their efforts to improve maternal and child health worldwide.

The A21 Campaign

The A21 Campaign exists to prevent human trafficking, protect those who have been trafficked, prosecute traffickers, and partner with local law enforcement to rescue those trapped in bondage. **theA21Campaign.org**

Abolition International

Abolition International is about bringing an end to sex trafficking and exploitation through education, empowerment, and comprehensive restorative care. **hopeforjustice.org**

Blood:Water

Blood:Water is an equipping agency that partners with African grassroots organizations to address the HIV/AIDS and water crises. **bloodwater.org**

Catholic Medical Mission Board (CMMB)

CMMB is the leading US-based Catholic charity focused exclusively on global health care, concentrating on making health care available to all, but particularly on the well-being of women and children in the developing world. **cmmb.org**

Children's AIDS Fund

The Children's AIDS Fund serves families, children, and orphans all over the world through HIV care and treatment and prevention. **childrensaidsfund.org**

Christian Connections for International Health (CCIH)

CCIH promotes international health and wholeness from a Christian perspective. **ccih.org**

Christian Medical and Dental Associations (CMDA)

CMDA motivates, educates, and equips Christian health care professionals to glorify God by serving with professional excellence as witnesses of Christ's love and compassion to all peoples, and advancing biblical principles of health care within the church and to our culture. **cmda.org**

Compassion International

Compassion International exists as a Christian child advocacy ministry that releases children from spiritual, economic, social, and physical poverty and enables them to become responsible, fulfilled Christian adults. **compassion.com**

Every Mother Counts

Every Mother Counts is a nonprofit organization dedicated to making pregnancy and childbirth safe for every mother. **everymothercounts.org**

Girls Not Brides

Girls Not Brides is a global partnership of more than 400 civil society organizations committed to ending child marriage and enabling girls to fulfill their potential. **girlsnotbrides.org**

LiveBeyond

LiveBeyond is a nonprofit humanitarian organization serving developing countries by building hospitals, purifying water, and making microfinance available. **mmdr.org**

Lwala Community Alliance

Lwala Community Alliance works to build the capacity of the people of Lwala, Kenya, to advance their own comprehensive well-being through health and development. **lwalacommunityalliance.org**

Save the Children

Save the Children is the world's top independent charity for children in need. They save children's lives and help them reach their full potential. **savethechildren.org**

Shalom Foundation

The Shalom Foundation's mission is to encourage Christian values by providing humanitarian assistance to children and their families living in extreme poverty. **theshalomfoundation.org**

Show Hope

The mission of Show Hope is to restore the hope of a family to children around the world who have been orphaned. showhope.org

United Methodist Committee on Relief

This committee is a nonprofit organization dedicated to alleviating human suffering around the globe. **umcor.org**

World Relief

As the compassionate service arm of the National Association of Evangelicals, World Relief is a nonprofit organization that provides humanitarian aid and disaster and emergency relief and is involved in community and economic development. **worldrelief.org**

World Vision

World Vision is a Christian humanitarian organization dedicated to working with children, families, and their communities worldwide to reach their full potential by tackling the causes of poverty and injustice. **worldvision.org**

Bibliography

Many of the statistics cited throughout this book are pulled from the following sources.

The Bill and Melinda Gates Foundation. "Family Planning." http://www.gatesfoundation.org/What-We-Do/Global-Development/Family-Planning

The Bill and Melinda Gates Foundation. "Maternal, Neonatal, and Child Health." http://www.gatesfoundation.org/What-We-Do/Global-Development/Maternal-Neonatal-and-Child-Health

Fuller, Jaime. "Hillary Clinton Says Equality for Women Is the 'Great Unfinished Business of the 21st Century.'" *The Washington Post.* March 7, 2014. http://www.washingtonpost.com/blogs/post-politics/wp/2014/03/07/hillary-clinton-says-equality-for-women-is-the-great-unfinished-business-of-the-21st-century/

International Labor Office. "Profits and Poverty: The Economics of Forced Labour." http://www.ilo.org/wcmsp5/groups/public/---ed_norm/---declaration/documents/publication/wcms_243391.pdf

Interpol. "Fact Sheet: Trafficking in Human Beings." 2013. http://www.interpol.int/Crime-areas/Trafficking-in-human-beings/Trafficking-in-human-beings

K4 Health. "Population Reports: Birth Spacing—Three to Five Saves Lives." https://www.k4health.org/sites/default/files/l13.pdf

Kanako Ishida, Paul Stupp, et al. "Ethnic Inequality in Guatemalan Women's Use of Modern Reproductive Health Care." *International Perspectives on Sexual and Reproductive Health,* June 2012. http://www.guttmacher.org/pubs/journals/3809912.html

Kristof, Nicholas D., and Sheryl WuDunn. *Half the Sky.* New York: Random House, 2009.

United Nations. "We Can End Poverty: Millennium Development Goals and Beyond 2015." http://www.un.org/millenniumgoals (click through to the UN Report PDF)

The United Nations Children's Fund (UNICEF). "Child Marriage." http://www.unicef.org/protection/57929_58008.html

United Nations Department of Economic and Social Affairs. "Sustainable Development Goals." http://sustainabledevelopment.un.org/?menu=1300

United Nations Development Programme. "Improve Maternal Health: Where Do We Stand?" http://www.undp.org/content/brussels/en/home/mdgoverview/mdg_goals/mdg5/

United Nations Population Fund. "Marrying Too Young." http://www.unfpa.org/public/home/publications/pid/12166

United Nations Population Fund. "Maternal Deaths Halved in 20 Years, but Faster Progress Needed." http://www.unfpa.org/public/home/news/pid/10730

United Nations Population Fund. "Maternal Health." http://www.unfpa.org/public/mothers/

World Health Organization. "Adolescent pregnancy." http://www.who.int/mediacentre/factsheets/fs364/en/

World Health Organization. "Obstetric Fistula: The Untreated Tragedy." http://www.who.int/reproductivehealth/topics/maternal_perinatal/fistula-study/en/

World Health Organization. "Why Do So Many Women Still Die in Pregnancy or Childbirth?" http://www.who.int/features/qa/12/en

HOPE

THROUGH HEALING HANDS

Hope Through Healing Hands is a nonprofit 501(c)3 whose mission is to promote an improved quality of life for citizens and communities around the world using health as a currency for peace.

Through the prism of health diplomacy, we envision a world where all individuals and families can obtain access to health care information, services, and support for the opportunity at a fuller life. Specifically, we seek sustainability through health care service and training.

This includes efforts for maternal, newborn, and child health; healthy timing and spacing of pregnancies; clean water; extreme poverty; emergency relief; and global diseases such as HIV/AIDS, tuberculosis, and malaria. Strategically, we encourage global health partnerships by working hand in hand with leading organizations that best address these issues in developing nations.

Follow us at:

www.HopeThroughHealingHands.org

@HTHHglobal on Twitter

www.facebook.com/HopeThroughHealingHands

THE FAITH-BASED COALITION FOR
Healthy Mothers & Children
WORLDWIDE

The Faith-Based Coalition for Healthy Mothers and Children Worldwide is a campaign of Hope Through Healing Hands to build a coalition of advocates who are speaking out about the struggles that mothers and children in developing nations face daily. For instance, over 287,000 women in developing nations die from preventable complications during pregnancy and childbirth, and 6.6 million children die from preventable causes before their fifth birthday each year. But we can change this. We seek to galvanize faith-based leaders and their constituencies around the issues of maternal, newborn, and child health (MNCH) as well as healthy timing and spacing of pregnancies (HTSP) to improve maternal health and reduce child mortality.

Our goal is to educate and activate thought-leaders to discuss, debate, and advocate on these issues, addressing MNCH and HTSP. Members of the coalition have varied positions on particular methods, which include fertility-awareness approaches as well as contraceptives, but all agree that healthy timing and spacing of pregnancies is imperative for saving the lives of women and children and enhancing the flourishing of families worldwide.

Join us to learn more about how you can become involved as an advocate for mothers and children. www.hopethroughhealinghands.org/faith-based-coalition

Mother & Child Project Discussion Guide

Raising Our Voices for Health and Hope

Foreword by Kay Warren; Preface by Melinda Gates; Compiled by Hope Through Healing Hands

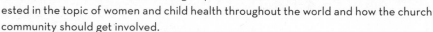

A discussion guide specifically written as a companion piece to *The Mother & Child Project* that will prompt helpful conversations for book clubs, small groups, and others interested in the topic of women and child health throughout the world and how the church community should get involved.

The discussion guide is divided into four sessions—one to complement each section of the book, *The Mother & Child Project*.

Each session is divided into two parts: "At Home"—several suggested essays to read from the book prior to the gathering to discuss—and "In Your Small Group"—several discussion questions, often supplemented by a pertinent quote from the book, plus a follow-up activity to become personally involved.

Available in stores and online!

ZONDERVAN®
.com